Grow What You Eat, Eat What You Grow

Grow What You Eat, Eat What You Grow

The Green Man's Guide to Living & Eating Sustainably All Year Round

Randy Shore

Arsenal Pulp Press
Vancouver

ARSENAL PULP PRESS
Suite 202–211 East Georgia St.
Vancouver, BC V6A 1Z6
Canada
arsenalpulp.com

The publisher gratefully acknowledges the support of the Government of Canada (through the Canada Book Fund) and the Government of British Columbia (through the Book Publishing Tax Credit Program) for its publishing activities.

The author and publisher assert that the information contained in this book is true and complete to the best of their knowledge. All recommendations are made without the guarantee on the part of the author and publisher. The author and publisher disclaim any liability in connection with the use of this information. For more information, contact the publisher.

Note for our UK readers: measurements for non-liquids are for volume, not weight.

Design by Gerilee McBride
All photographs by Tracey Kusiewicz/Foodie Photography except for the following: Gerilee McBride (pp. 6, 8, 15, 19, 20–22, 24–25, 28, 64, 66 bottom, 68, 70, 72 bottom, 73 top, 89, 95, 105, 116, 122–23, 127, 168, 177, 201, 215); Randy Shore (pp. 33, 66 top, 71, 73 bottom, 81, 97)
Editing by Susan Safyan

Printed and bound in Canada

Library and Archives Canada Cataloguing in Publication:

Shore, Randy, 1963–, author
     Grow what you eat, eat what you grow: the Green Man's guide to living & eating sustainably all year round / Randy Shore.

Includes index.
Issued in print and electronic formats.
ISBN 978-1-55152-548-8 (pbk.).
—ISBN 978-1-55152-549-5 (epub)

     1. Vegetable gardening—Canada. 2. Kitchen gardens—Canada. 3. Vegetables—Preservation. 4. Cooking (Vegetables). I. Title.

SB323.C3S56 2014   635'.0971
C2014-905409-2

C2014-905410-6

Contents

Introduction

*How to Grow What You Eat
and Eat What You Grow*

I want you to stop and quiet your mind. Turn off the television, the radio, your smartphone, and whatever else you are using to stay connected to every other human being on the planet. Now, bite into an apple or a strawberry or a tomato and consider where it came from, how it got to you, and what it tastes like.

This is a revolutionary act in our culture: We aren't supposed to think about where things come from and how they are grown. The shelves of our grocery stores are piled high with fruits and vegetables from somewhere, ready-to-eat foods made by someone. We don't often question these things because we are accustomed to seeing every imaginable food—in abundance— every day of the year.

The average grocery store has about 40,000 different food products in stock. You just tasted one. What did you think? If it was a tomato or a winter strawberry from California or Mexico, it probably didn't taste like much at all. Fruits and vegetables have been selectively bred to be stable for transport, not for flavor. Ready-to-eat foods are the food industry's clever way of making crops such as corn or soy beans into commodities that are bought and sold by the ton. A large and very efficient food industry turns those commodities into products that can be packaged for a long shelf life. Ad men may even have you convinced that you don't have time to cook from fresh ingredients.

I think you do have time to cook, but for a

spring

summer

autumn

winter

variety of reasons—from information fatigue to over-scheduling to a simple lack of confidence— you may choose not to. And moreover, I believe you have time to grow at least some of your own food. In the world of plants, seeds and sun do all the heavy lifting. If you can poke a seed into a pot of soil, you will be rewarded. A seed can return more than a thousand times its weight in fresh food for a very modest investment of time and energy.

Growing food and cooking it yourself minutes after harvest ensures peak nutritional value. Most so-called fresh vegetables lose half their vitamins and antioxidants in the days that it takes to travel from field to fork. The physiological benefits of gardening and cooking are many, but the psychological benefits may be even greater.

A few years ago, I wanted to create a place where food mattered, where the earth mattered, where I could start to feel good again after years of grinding commutes, rushed meals, and thoughtless consumption. I moved my somewhat reluctant wife Darcy and two sons out of the city to an acre in a neighborhood of acreages. My move was dramatic, but yours doesn't have to be. You can take small but still important steps toward a more fulfilled, flavorful life without selling your house or leaving the city.

The best thing that I do each day is walk through my yard looking for dinner. Even in the rain, it's more fulfilling than commuting, talking to my boss, or answering email. It slows me down, quiets my mind, and gets me focused on what I'm going to cook and eat that night. If I want to, I can look for what might be ripe and ready for tomorrow, too. Or I can make that tomorrow's adventure.

I have a large garden, but that is not a

prerequisite for deliberate eating. You can do the same thing at a farmer's market or by looking over pots of fresh herbs on your apartment balcony. You can reconnect with food, with the land, and with your family by choosing, cooking, and eating food together. If this sounds a bit fanciful and poetic, it's no accident. Poetry is meant to make you feel—and I think that eating food that you have grown yourself and cooked simply, but with care, will make you feel nourished and happy and connected. Even if all you grow is parsley in a pot on your windowsill, it will smell more pungent and taste fresher than whatever wilted bunches you can find in the grocery store. The fragrance of my fresh-cut herbs runs through my brain and down my spine with waves of pleasure. I always, always, stop to smell the herbs.

Balcony gardens can easily supply a few salads a week and all the fresh herbs two people could hope to use. Most suburban yards are full of sunny sheltered spots for pots and underutilized lawn that is easily made productive. My neighbors in Vancouver, for example, grew hundreds of garlic bulbs in their front yard rather than planting a lawn. Many city dwellers are doing likewise, taking control of their personal health and the health of their urban environment by swapping turf for kale and cauliflower, plants that are as decorative as they are edible.

A garden is your trip to the gym, your free-food grocery store, and a potent source of vitamins, fiber, and antioxidants all rolled into one.

When I set myself the task of growing my own food, a million things ran through my mind. Could I go off the grid and thumb my nose at the grocery store and Big Food? Would I save money? Lose weight? Or would I grow lettuce for forty dollars a head? I embarked on a quest to eat something that I grew myself, every day, for one year. Eating home-grown food twelve months of the year requires diligence and skill— skill I did not, at first, possess. I had no idea what I was getting into and soon found myself as transformed as the raw land from which I had carved my garden.

Darcy and I began curing, canning, and freezing. Old family recipes were dusted off, many of them scrawled on index cards with scant instructions. I started seedlings in my office and grew alfalfa and mung bean sprouts in the kitchen. I built a greenhouse, then a shed for potting and drying everything from dill and coriander seeds to potatoes and onions. I searched the yard for spaces to exploit in winter, early spring, and late fall, in an effort to produce fresh food outside the normal growing season. For every soggy or sandy, hard-to-manage bit of ground in your yard, there are sunny nooks, warm south-facing walls, and protected patio spaces that can produce food in a pot of soil, sometimes year-round.

Five years later, I am still very much on the grid. Darcy still visits the grocery store regularly (though usually without me, as I am "disruptive"). I guess I didn't really expect to grow all my own food while holding down a demanding job writing for a major daily newspaper, blogging about cooking and gardening, and debunking nutrition myths for television. I underestimated the skill set required to farm even a quarter of an acre.

My father grew up on a farm, but none of that generational knowledge was passed down to me. So when my first radishes sprouted and died, I had no idea why. For every happy success came a confusing failure. Every vegetable has its own preferences for soil, water, sunlight, and nutrients. Every yard has a completely unique set of microclimates and soil conditions. I learned about soil and composting, the basics of which can be mastered with a little trial and error (more on that later). I am still learning the intricacies of my property and, over time, you too will become the world's leading expert at growing food in yours.

Planning the garden and our meals—harvesting, processing, pickling, cooking, and eating our own food—is what Darcy and I do together every single day.

Today, the spare room is full of cured onions in cardboard boxes and the extra dresser loaded with Yukon Gold and Warba potatoes. Darcy's mother and grandmother still remembered how to make pickles. They shared their recipes with us and even showed us how to do it. The pantry is stacked with dill and bread-and-butter pickles, jam, relish, and beets in jars. The freezer is well-stocked with tomatoes for sauce and dozens of vacuum-sealed bags of green, yellow, and purple bush beans. In season, we always have a good supply of spinach, chard, three kinds of kale, four kinds of lettuce, carrots, turnips, and fresh herbs. Tomatoes, hot and mild peppers, zucchini, pattypan squash, and other sub-tropicals thrive during the summer, if I give them a good start in the house.

Cookbooks written over the past four decades assume that you have access to every imaginable ingredient in the world—which you do, at the grocery store. But most modern cookbooks pay little attention to the kinds of fruits and vegetables that people can and do grow themselves or find at the local farmer's market. This book condenses five years of experimentation into 130-plus recipes and includes seasonal tips for growing your own food. The recipes are designed to use the produce that you can easily grow yourself, in simple, delicious, and sustainable ways. The gardening instructions are intended to help you make use of every bit of ground and every favorable microclimate in your yard and home to produce food. Traditional farmhouse methods—canning, pickling, and preserving—are dusted off and modernized for the twenty-first century cook.

Let's take it season by season, prepare the soil, reap the bounty, and prepare tasty, nourishing food. You can grow what you eat and eat what you grow. You can slow down, unplug, and feel better.

Randy Shore

Spring

Plan, then Plant

I ache to get out in the garden in the first days of spring, to smell the soil, feel my muscles, weed, hoe, till, and build raised beds. But I don't.

Do I gaze longingly out my window? Yes. But I resist the urge to work cold, wet soil. Mucking around in the garden before the soil has warmed and given up some of its winter moisture can turn your growing space into a mixture not unlike concrete. Clods of compacted earth can take up to a year to break down and make weeding all but impossible.

If you get a break in the rain and a string of sunny days in early spring, you can plant peas and broad beans without doing too much harm to your soil structure. Choose the sunniest spot in the garden—the spot where you will put your tomatoes at the beginning of summer—such as the space in front of a south-facing fence or wall. Put the broad beans in close to the fence and plant a row of peas immediately in front of them, to the south. You don't want your peas trapped in the shade of broad-bean stalks that can easily top four feet (1.2 m). Now, walk away.

The first few weeks of spring are for mapping your yard's productive zones and planning your crops. I want you to reimagine your yard as a miniature farm. For this task, you will need a few sheets of graph paper, a pencil, and a compass. A current seed catalog will come in handy as well.

Draw a large outline of your entire lot on the graph paper and then add the outline of the house. Add the sun decks, flower beds, balconies, sidewalks, and driveway. Put in the trees and the outline of the garden, if it exists, or where you'd like your garden to be, if it doesn't yet exist. Get out your compass and label your map with North, South, East, and West.

Pick a sunny day in the last two weeks of March and go out in the yard around nine a.m. Mark the areas on your map that are in the shade. Repeat this exercise at three p.m. (Depending on where the buildings and trees are in your yard, you might want to try it at ten a.m. and four p.m.) Now, look at what is left. The unshaded areas of your yard—the spaces that are in full sun between nine a.m. and three p.m.—are the most potentially productive. The other spaces aren't useless, but they are trickier to use effectively, or they may be suitable for certain crops. Cilantro, for instance, likes cool morning sun but prefers shade in the afternoon. Thyme and rosemary thrive in hot afternoon sun.

South-facing walls, fences, and sundecks reflect heat and light and provide some shelter from the wind, creating sub-tropical microclimates suitable for tomatoes, basil, peppers, and eggplant vines. Like a cloche or cold frame, a simple lean-to frame made of wood and covered with clear plastic can magnify the effect.

This heat map, as crude as it may be, is an invaluable tool for deciding where different types of vegetables, each with different needs, should be positioned to thrive. Wild plants are both competitors and specialists, built to exploit particular conditions of moisture, fertility, light, and warmth. Vegetables are selectively bred to bring out certain characteristics such as large edible roots or succulent leafy greens. They are not built to compete; rather, they depend on you to give them everything they need and defend them from anything that will interfere with their ability to convert elemental nutrients and sunshine into food. You and your vegetables are partners, but you are the brains of the operation.

Consider container gardening. Pots of soil act like little microclimates, warming the roots of plants whenever the sun comes out. Pots warm much faster than the soil in your garden, giving you a minimum one-month head start on planting. Because they are portable, pots can also be moved to wherever the sun is that week and follow it around the yard as the seasons progress. By choosing the sunniest locations in your yard for containers, you can start seedlings for transplanting far earlier than it would be possible to sow seeds directly in the garden.

Raised beds do much the same work in the garden, promoting solar heat gain, drainage, and aeration, and allowing cool air to flow away in the channels between the boxes or raised sections. To grow food successfully in the spring, you need to learn your yard's secret hot spots to optimize growing conditions.

THE SOIL IS A LIVING THING

The soil in your garden is a living thing—actually, billions of living things. Minerals, organic matter, and microbiota, in balance, provide the elemental nutrients that plants need to grow. You've probably seen the Big Three listed on the front of fertilizer packages as N-P-K: nitrogen, phosphorus, and potassium. Each number (e.g., 3-15-0) is the percentage of the nutrient by weight. Chemical fertilizers provide those elements but in quantities that can unleash a massive burst of energy, literally burning the organic matter right out of your soil.

Vegetables need those elemental nutrients—along with many other micronutrients such as copper, manganese, zinc, iron, and magnesium—to grow. But they need them over the long haul, not just for a day or a few weeks.

Microbes will eat your chemical fertilizers, but the effect will not often be what you desire. Think about a campfire, burning low and slow. Feed it slowly with wood, and it stays at a nice temperature for a long time, releasing energy at a rate that is useful for cooking. If you use gasoline on the campfire, you will release loads of heat, but in a flash, which is not useful for cooking. Microbial activity releases energy and nutrients like embers release heat—low and slow.

The temperature of your soil will rise through the spring until the peak of summer, and the growth rate of your plants will increase along with it. As soil temperatures rise, microbial activity will increase in the soil too, conveniently releasing energy and nutrients as your plants require them. Your job is to carefully stoke the microbial fire in your soil with good fuel. Well-rotted compost and manures will provide long-burning fuel, and the process of adding them will cause your metaphorical fire to flare up—briefly—and then settle down.

When you load your garden with nutritious manures and compost and aerate the soil in the process, the microbes are going to have a party, burning nitrogen and oxygen like there's no tomorrow and making the soil's nutrients temporarily unavailable to plants. Wait a few weeks for the party to die down and plant when the soil has settled down—low and slow.

MAKE YOUR OWN CUSTOM FERTILIZERS

I mix my own fertilizer for a variety of reasons. I like the idea of using agricultural byproducts like seed and bone meals rather than manufactured nutrients. It's a circle-of-life thing. I also like to tweak the mix to match the needs of plants that want a little more of one thing than the other, especially spinach (nitrogen), potatoes (calcium), and tomatoes (phosphorus).

The mix becomes active as the soil warms up, triggering a complex set of biological processes that make the nutrients available in a form that your vegetables can easily consume. Bone meal, kelp meal, blood meal, and lime are available at any good garden center. Seed meals (such as alfalfa or canola) are used for animal feed, so you may have to consult a farm-supply business to find them. Don't be afraid to buy a big bag—it's cheap. My acre of garden goes through ninety lb (forty kg) a year.

The nutritional values of my fertilizer components break down as follows:

Seed meal: Alfalfa, soy, cottonseed, and canola meal offer slow-release nitrogen and phosphorus with a trace of potassium. I use canola seed meal because it's the cheapest, but alfalfa meal is sometimes easier to find. N-P-K: 4-1-1

Bone meal: Use steamed or dolomite bone meal to provide slow-release phosphorus for root development with the bonus of calcium, which your dark greens will like. Nitrogen content varies by brand. N-P-K: 3-15-0

Kelp meal: This dry fertilizer is lower in nitrogen but higher in potassium than seed meals and an important source of trace minerals, such as copper, zinc, and magnesium. N-P-K: 1-0-3.

Compost: Well-rotted compost improves aeration in clay soils and improves moisture retention in sandy soils. N-P-K: 1-1-1.

Blood meal: I don't put blood meal in my general-purpose mix, but it provides a quick hit of nitrogen when slow-release isn't enough. N-P-K: 14-0-0.

Lime: Coastal soils are quite acidic, which can interfere with nutrient absorption, while inland soils are often more balanced with little need for lime. Buy a test kit or check with local experts on your neighborhood's soil conditions. Lime reduces acidity in sandy soils and may improve the structure of clay soils.

If you are gardening in a small space or balcony, buy fertilizer components with a neighbor and split them, like my mom does.

If you keep the components of your fertilizer separate, you can mix on-the-fly for each bed of vegetables you plant (while keeping careful notes on its effect, of course). Here are some examples:

Basic Fertilizer Mix

10 parts canola seed or alfalfa meal
1 part bone meal
1 part kelp meal
1 part dolomite lime*

Potato Fertilizer Mix

2 parts seed meal
1 part kelp meal
1 part bone meal

Spinach Fertilizer Mix

6 parts seed meal
1 part kelp meal
1 part bone meal
1 part dolomite lime*
$\frac{1}{10}$ part blood meal

If soil pH is below 6.0

For vigorous plant growth, hoe in the fertilizer mix when you plant a row of seeds or put a few tablespoons in the hole before you plant seedlings. I use about 1 cup (250 mL) for every two yd/m of row, and double that for onions. For plants that grow very large, such as cauliflower, incorporate about ½ cup (125 mL) under each seedling.

I use Basic Fertilizer Mix when I till in cover crops or shredded leaves to expedite decomposition, firing up the microbes to do their work. Spread a light dusting of fertilizer over the weeds, shredded leaves, clover, fall rye, or whatever other cover crops you have, and till it in.

The Basic Fertilizer Mix is also useful as a compost accelerator. If I want to build a fast compost heap for use within a few months (as opposed to my usual two years), I will use shredded leaves in alternating layers with green garden waste that I have chopped to ribbons with a machete. Dust each layer with a handful of fertilizer and dampen it with the water hose to jump-start decomposition. If you get it right, the heap should get hot enough inside to kill all the weed seeds. Turn and mix the heap every few weeks to aerate and reignite decomposition.

WHAT ARE YOU GOING TO GROW?

Deciding what crops you are going to grow is one part personal taste and one part rational analysis. In other words, you must reconcile what you want to eat from the garden with what you can reasonably expect to grow with success. Even veteran gardeners experience crop failures, and it can take years to figure out exactly what went wrong. Climate, soil quality, nutrient levels, pests, and the vagaries of each season's weather are only the most obvious of the limitless variables with which you will contend each and every year. And conditions will change each and every year.

Garden crops fall into three general categories: Things you really want to grow, things you can easily grow, and things it makes financial sense to grow.

Take a fresh piece of paper and make three columns. In the first column, list two or three vegetables that you absolutely love. For me, there is no point in gardening at all if I don't grow tomatoes. The difference between a tart, sweet, juicy garden tomato and the flavorless, uniform grocery store product is immeasurable. It's what gets me out of bed in the morning. I round out the first column with Thai Dragon chilies and green onions.

In the second column, list the vegetables that are virtually fool-proof, prolific, and unlikely to succumb to pests. Peas, beans, spinach, chard, kale, zucchini, and lettuce grow vigorously in most soils, require relatively little space for the amount of food they produce and thrive even if the weather is less than perfect. If you have a large garden, add potatoes and storage onions to the second column. Neither is expensive to buy, but they are extraordinarily productive in terms of calories delivered for the area they require, and both store well, so you'll be eating them right through the winter.

In the third column, list your favorite herbs and pricey veggies. Fresh herbs deliver a ton of flavor and a big hit of antioxidants and vitamins. They are expensive to buy but easy to grow, so it makes sense to grow them yourself. In fact, if you grow nothing else, grow herbs.

Choose from sage, rosemary, thyme, chives, and oregano, all of which require a permanent home in your yard. If you can, create an herb garden on the south side of the house and as near the kitchen as possible. (During rainy weather, the shorter the trip between the kitchen and your herbs the better.) They will all thrive in large pots on a sunny deck or balcony. Parsley, basil, cilantro, and dill can also be grown in containers or in the garden, but you must sow them anew each spring. One bay laurel shrub will supply you and your neighbors with fresh bay leaves year-round. Baby carrots, cherry tomatoes, and broccoli can all be expensive to buy, so it might make sense to also add them to column three.

If you have children who want to grow their own Jack-o'-lanterns, consider a pumpkin vine—although, at about seventeen cents per lb (500 g), it's not a very wise use of garden space. Sweet corn is also a space hog, and you can buy it in season by the side of the road for a pittance. To me, it's not worth the trouble.

Use the list to guide your study of a good regional seed catalog and to help you make good choices at the garden center.

GET A HEAD START

Seeds are cheap. You can buy 1,000 onion seeds for about fifteen dollars. Carrot and lettuce seeds are even cheaper. I am willing to risk a dollar for the possibility of spring salads. If your seeds sprout and you get a late frost, I'm sorry to say you gambled and lost. Hey, it was only a buck.

There are quite a few plants that you can sow in three- or five-gallon pots in a sunny, sheltered part of the yard a week or two before the estimated date of your last frost of the spring. In warmer regions, that could be as early as March 10, but for gardeners in colder climes, as late as mid-May. Watch the weather forecast. If you are worried about a late frost, throw a sheet of clear plastic over your seeded pots for extra protection during the first few weeks after you sow your seeds, then remove it.

Use commercial garden mix or potting soil for container gardening and starting seeds. The naturally occurring pests and pathogens in garden soil will spring to life when it warms up and can sicken or devour your seedlings. The following greens are generally successful early starters:

- **Arugula** is a bitter green that will grow quite happily in containers in the yard or on a balcony, and it can remain productive right through the summer if it gets afternoon shade. Mix ½ cup (125 mL) Spinach Fertilizer Mix (p. 14) with soil in a five-gallon container. Pick a sunny, sheltered location and sow eight to ten seeds. Arugula may take one or two weeks to germinate, depending on the temperature. One month after they sprout, feed with high-nitrogen fish fertilizer. Harvest the larger outside leaves and mix with mild lettuce to add a peppery punch to salads.

- **Parsley** is a cousin of the carrot that has a large root system. Sow parsley in 4-inch containers of potting soil and transplant to the garden when they are six inches tall. If you intend to keep parsley in a container or balcony garden, use a five-gallon pot. Mix 1 cup (250 mL) Basic Fertilizer Mix (p. 14) into the soil and sow the seeds about ¼-inch (6-mm) deep. Be patient; parsley can take a full month to germinate. The plants will thrive in full sun but also tolerate afternoon shade. When you harvest, take leaves and stems from the outside, leaving the new shoots in the center of the plant intact.

- **Spinach** has a relatively compact root system and will grow to maturity in pots. Make sure to harvest and retire the plant before the hot weather comes in summer, because spinach bolts easily. Spinach sown late in August can be productive until the first frost. For container cultivation, mix three gallons of soil with ½ cup (125 mL) of Spinach Fertilizer Mix (p. 14). Seed transplants in 4-inch pots and move them into the garden after the first true leaves appear.

- **Mizuna** is a crisp Japanese salad green with spiky, slightly bitter leaves. Mizuna will grow no matter what the weather dishes up. Even in a cold, wet summer, when your sun-loving veggies are dreaming of California, your mizuna will carry the mail. Prepare a five-gallon pot with 1 cup (250 mL) Basic Fertilizer Mix (p. 14) and plant four or five seeds. The plants are prolific and resist bolting. For transplants, plant two seeds per 4-inch pot and thin to a single plant about two weeks before moving to the garden.

- **Chives** are perfect for balconies and pots as they tend to spread quickly when not contained. They grow abundantly at the first kiss of spring sunshine. Prepare a three-gallon container with soil and ½ cup (125 mL) of Spinach Fertilizer Mix (p. 14). Sow chives up to four weeks before the last frost and the seeds will come up as soon as the soil warms. Chives die back in the winter and rebound every spring, barring a deep, hard frost. As insurance, in August collect 1 tbsp of seeds from the dried flowers and set them aside, just in case.

PREPARE THE GARDEN

In spring, my garden is a mix of permanent beds of asparagus and herbs—sage, rosemary, thyme, and oregano—that occupy the same space year-round, as well as overwintered chard and kale, and cover crops such as fall rye, field peas, and oats. At least two beds are dedicated to garlic planted the previous October and mulched with 6 in (15 cm) of shredded leaves. Any space not taken up with permanent installations, cover crops, and overwintering crops, I cover with leaf mulch for the winter. In other words, there are a lot of moving parts, and each has different needs.

Preparing garden soil for planting is an exercise in patience. If you have a cover crop in place, it should leap back to life and put on significant growth as the soil temperature rises. That's a good thing. Legumes and grasses have deep, elaborate root networks that drag nutrients from deep in the soil and store them. When you till in the cover crop, the tops and roots decompose and release all those nutrients close to the surface, in the root zone of your vegetables.

The trick with cover crops is to allow them to put on fast growth as the weather warms and till them in before they toughen. Mature grasses form lignin and cellulose, fibers that are hard to break up with a tiller or a hoe. Tough grasses and stems are also very slow to decompose. Check cover crop grasses for tenderness often at this time of year and turn them under quickly when they start to toughen.

Once the last frost has passed, a string of sunny, dry weather could warm the soil enough to till and to work in compost. Use a shovel to remove the top 6 in (15 cm) of soil and grab a handful. Squeeze it in your hand. If it forms a ball that crumbles when you poke it, the soil is safe to work. Be honest with yourself. If it's too early, don't risk it.

> **Be sure to date your yard map after you write in the locations of each crop. Save every year's map so you can rotate crops around the garden the next year to discourage pests from accumulating.**

Before tilling, lightly dust your cover crops and leaf mulch with Basic Fertilizer Mix (p. 14) to speed decomposition. Take care not to use lime in the area of the garden where you intend to plant potatoes. Use the Potato Fertilizer Mix (p. 14) for that space.

A tilled-in cover crop—what farmers call green manure—takes about three to four weeks to decompose, if the weather is favorable. After three weeks, if your garden is particularly weedy, you may want to till a second time to eradicate more of the weeds and kill any that have sprouted from newly exposed seeds. Weed seeds can lurk in the soil for years, just waiting to be moved close enough to the surface to sprout. While you are waiting for the green manure to do its thing, you can prepare some necessary infrastructure and take a few important measurements.

In a perfect world, your garden would be slightly higher than the surrounding landscape and slope gently to the south. Depressions allow cold air to pool, creating persistent pockets of frost until late in the spring, delaying germination and slowing plant growth. Building raised beds or boxed gardens above the grade of the surrounding land helps, but terraforming to create optimal conditions should be your long-term goal.

Get out your compass, a long piece of lumber such as a two-by-four, and a carpenter's level. Place the two-by-four on the garden soil pointing north-south and place the level on top. If the level indicates that your garden is generally flat or sloping to the south—happy days. Cold air flows down, but it will remain trapped where it cannot drain away.

In wine country, grape growers prize south-facing slopes and will spend large sums of money to fill in depressions and create channels for cold air drainage. You can do the same, but without spending large sums of money. As you build your garden's soil, fill in depressions, raise the garden above the grade of the rest of the yard, and create a gentle slope, high to the north and low to the south. It may take years to achieve, but every square foot of your garden will be more productive.

IT'S TIME TO PLANT

If you live near the West Coast, spring may be long and wet but seldom freezing cold, and the transition from winter to summer will be about three months long. That means you can plant quick, cool-weather crops to harvest before your summer vegetables, such as tomatoes and peppers, go in the ground. Plant early crops in the sunniest locations when the danger of frost has passed, and plan to devote that space over to the heat lovers come June or July.

Inland, your last frost might come just weeks before summer starts, so you need to set aside the right locations for heat-loving plants right from the start. You won't have time to get cool-weather crops to maturity in less than six weeks, with the possible exception of radishes.

Good regional seed suppliers provide local guidance on planting dates for your area, either in their catalogs or on their seed packets. Use that information and your local knowledge. Every garden is different, so you have to make yourself an expert on your growing space. Keep notes about each crop that you plant, noting the date you sow, where it is in the garden, and how successfully it grows. Experiment with your fertilizer mix too.

Pull out your carefully drawn yard map and your list of vegetables to make a rough plan for planting and succession. Early-season crops like radishes, spinach, kale, peas, and broad beans go in first. There is no rule that says you have to fill your entire garden with seeds and plants in one weekend. That strategy guarantees you will be overrun with produce when all those plants mature. Plant a little bit each week, and you will produce vegetables in manageable amounts over a longer period of time.

Draw some boxes on the garden space on your map and consider which vegetables from your list you want to grow and in what quantity. In a smaller garden, opt for high-value crops, the ones you can't live without and the ones that are expensive to buy. If you have a large garden space, you can devote space to storage crops such as potatoes and onions. As a general rule, place taller crops to the north and lower plants to the south, so everybody gets a look at the sun.

Here are a few tips to guide your thinking:

- **Tomato vines** can easily reach 6 ft (1.8 m) tall if they are staked and carefully pruned. Place them in full sun on the north edge of the garden to avoid throwing shade on other crops. A combination of early and late varieties will prevent a glut of fruit at any one time during the growing season. One vine of sauce tomatoes, such as San Marzano, can easily produce more than 100 pieces of fruit. In a good season, four San Marzano vines can fill your freezer.

- **Spinach** wilts down to one-tenth of its volume when cooked. You will fill a bucket to get just four portions. Plan to plant 10 row ft (3 m) about every three weeks in spring for a continuous supply.

- **Bright Lights chard** is as prolific as it is colorful. Harvest leaves from the outside of the plant and it will produce six to ten months of the year. Half a dozen plants should be plenty for a family of four.

- **Cucumbers** produce prodigiously for about six weeks. Plant two vines of slicing cucumbers for a small family, four if you intend to make Bread-and-Butter Pickles (p. 131). Six vines of pickling cucumbers will net a two-year supply of Classic Dill Pickles (p. 132).

- Many **leaf lettuces** are cut-and-come-again, so half a dozen plants should be enough. For head lettuce and romaine, plant a few seeds every other week throughout the spring. If you plant twenty seeds at once, you will have twenty heads of lettuce to eat in one week at mid-summer.

- **Parsley** will grow 2 or 3 ft (61 cm to 1 m) high when let loose in the garden. Six big plants will give you a big handful of parsley every day throughout the growing season and possibly all winter too, if you are lucky with the weather.

- **Thyme, rosemary, chives, and sage** need a permanent location that offers some protection from the elements during the winter. Oregano may also overwinter in mild climates.

- **Asparagus** can thrive in the same location for ten to twenty years, so think long-term when you decide whether and where to grow it. (For more details on growing asparagus, see p. 67.)

- **Carrots** are delicious at any size, so plant your entire season's supply about a month after the last frost. Harvest baby carrots at about six weeks to thin the row and allow space for the other carrots to grow large. Plant carrots for autumn around the end of July.

- **Onions** are a staple at my house. I plant about 500 storage onions—both red and Spanish—and another twenty green onion seeds a week to eat young. To start storage onions, plant twenty seeds in 4-inch pots and transfer to the garden when they are 6 in (15 cm) tall.

- **Potatoes** are another of my big crops. I love them small as new potatoes and store enough mature keepers to last until spring. Once you've allotted space to your other crops, plant potatoes in the areas that are left vacant.

- **Dill and cilantro** provide tender, pungent herbs through the summer, then seeds to cook with through the winter and to re-sow next spring. Plant some seeds in a cool, moist location for succulent leaves and plant another handful in a hot, sunny location and let them go to seed.

 To plant radishes, loosen the soil to a depth of 3–4 inches (7.6–10 cm), then take a length of one-by-two and press it firmly into the soil. Plant the seeds on the compressed soil and cover with ½ inch (1 cm) compost. Compressing the soil will allow moisture to wick up from underneath, resulting in successful germination. Keep radishes moist at all times.

 To perk up sage and rosemary bushes in spring, brush away loose material on top of the soil over the roots and work in 1 cup (250 mL) Basic Fertilizer Mix (p. 14), then mulch with brown leaves or wood chips to suppress weeds.

ACTIVE AND PASSIVE SLUG CONTROL

Slugs are a menace any time plants are growing, but the damage they do to small, defenseless seedlings borders on criminal. These voracious monsters can wipe out an entire row of baby lettuce in one night. To control slugs, you must start early and be relentless. Every slug that is allowed to procreate can give rise to three dozen more of its kind in as little as ten days.

There are as many ways to control slugs as there are chatty neighbors with a lousy grasp of science. Nearly every solution is imperfect in some way, but hey, it's an imperfect world.

Seed catalogs offer expensive copper mesh or wire that you can use to surround your tender plants. Slugs do not like to cross metal barriers. But copper is an expensive solution and it doesn't kill them; it just encourages the slugs to find a way around or choose to eat something else.

Metaldehyde pellets are also a common and effective solution to controlling slugs, and the poison does kill them. It will also kill your puppy and your neighbor's cat. Metaldehyde causes kidney damage, liver damage, and even death in mammals—including pets and toddlers. If you use metaldehyde in the garden, you will end up eating it in trace amounts. I prefer to eat food without chemical pesticides, so I'm not about to use them in the garden.

Diatomaceous earth is a fine abrasive grit made from fossilized algae. You can purchase it at the garden center, but make sure you get a nontoxic food-grade type. If you drizzle a line of it around your plants, slugs will avoid it or be fatally injured. My concern with diatomaceous earth is that it will damage virtually every insect that crosses it, including the ladybugs that keep aphids and leaf miners under control. I don't use it.

A ring of dry, used coffee grounds around your tender seedlings may deter slugs from crossing, but it doesn't kill them. At worst, you will build your soil with the coffee grounds and repel ants and cats, so it's a no-lose solution. Dry coffee grounds on a sheet of plywood in the garage or shed and sprinkle them liberally around tender transplants.

I have read that slugs love rolled oats and will choose to eat them over your plants. The problem is that rats like them, too. Sorry, I'm not going to start feeding rats to control slugs.

Beer traps are an effective, passive form of slug control. Dig a few pie plates into the ground so they are level with the grade of the soil and fill them with stale beer. Beer attracts, traps, and kills the slugs, but I always step in the pans and wreck them, and then I have to clean up the gooey slug soup.

My preferred solution is the most labor-intensive, but it is also the cheapest and most effective. Take an old piece of plywood and cut it into strips 1 ft (30.5 cm) wide by 4 ft (1.2 m) long. Two or three of these is enough for a large garden. Lay the boards in the pathways and between the plants in the evenings, leaving a little space underneath. The next morning, when the sun is high in the sky, flip the boards over. Most of the local slug community will be waiting for you underneath or stuck on the boards themselves. Now you must terminate their lives, with extreme prejudice. A pinch of table salt will kill slugs quickly. I have a friend who stomps on them while uttering a deafening karate scream, which also works. It's up to you.

HOW TO GROW POTATOES

No vegetable suffers from more conflicting advice than the potato. People grow them in all sorts of contraptions, from plastic bags to used tires, and in the garden with techniques from trenching to heaping. A five-gallon planter will fill with potatoes over three months, if you can't find room to grow them in the garden.

My father grew potatoes by placing a seed potato on top of the garden soil and putting a spare tire around it. He then filled in the tire with soil as the vines grew higher, and added another tire and more soil as needed. This works, but you end up with a hole in the garden where all that soil used to be. I suppose if you have a big pile of soil just sitting around, you could try the tire method. I've also seen it done with stacked wood frames.

I've been growing potatoes for a few years now, and I have come to believe that the potato is so confident in its abilities, so resilient and so naturally prolific, that it will produce a crop no matter what method you use. That said, you can take some steps to ensure a good crop.

The reason the tire method works is that all the potatoes grow above the seed, none below. The object of the potato-growing exercise is to get as much loose fertile soil over the seed potato as possible.

Here's what I do: Grow oats on the potato patch the previous fall. Oats die in the deep frosts of winter and leave plenty of organic root material behind in the soil as well as dry, half-rotted oat straw on the surface of the soil.

Deeply work the entire bed with two-year-old compost. Avoid fresh manure, which may contain viruses and other pathogens. Avoid using lime on the potato patch for at least six months to one year before planting. I usually plant potatoes in newer soil, as I expand the footprint of the garden. Potatoes are reputedly very good at conditioning new soil.

Dig wells or a row trough about 1 ft (30.5 cm) deep. Each seed potato should have at least three eyes or sprouts. If your potato has six, cut it in half so there are three on each section. Place one seed potato at the bottom of the well every 24 in (61 cm) with the sprouts pointing up. Dust the surface of the soil around each seed with ½ cup (125 mL) Potato Fertilizer Mix (p. 14).

Using a hoe, gently pull loose soil and oat straw over the seed until it is buried about 2 in (5 cm) deep. Each time the vines get to be about 1 ft (30.5 cm) tall—once a month or so—pull more soil, straw, and dried leaves around them until the well fills in and then begin to create a hill around each vine.

The benefit of this method is that you don't have to weed the potato patch. Just use a sharp hoe to scrape the soil each time you heap it up and the weeds will be cut and recommit their stolen nutrients to the cause.

A week before planting, spread seed potatoes on a cookie sheet or short-sided cardboard box and place in a bright, but not sunny, window for a week. This will get the vines started.

About Salt

Throughout this collection of recipes, you will note that I use a variety of salts, especially kosher, sea, and pickling. You will never see ordinary table salt in my kitchen.

Kosher salt contains no added iodine and has a slightly larger grain than table salt. It has a neutral flavor and provides consistent, predictable seasoning.

Grey salt is harvested from the ocean in Brittany. This moist, organic salt is much coarser than table salt and is lower in sodium, but rich in magnesium, calcium, potassium, copper, iron, and zinc. Its mineral flavor profile is excellent with raw foods.

Pickling salt, sometimes called coarse salt, must be used in preserving. If you substitute other kinds of salt, it will dangerously alter the chemistry of the brine, resulting in inedible food—or worse.

Fresh Herb Chimichurri

Chimichurri is sometimes called Argentinian steak sauce, but this pungent little pesto is going to leave any steak sauce you ever tried in the dust. The combination of cilantro and parsley for herbaceous freshness, olive oil for a silky feel, and a little splash of red wine vinegar for tartness make this a gobsmacking experience. Serve with grilled meats, eggs, or just about anything else.

MAKES 1 CUP (250 ML)

¼ cup (125 mL) cilantro

½ cup (125 mL) flat-leaf parsley

2 tbsp fresh oregano

¼ cup (60 mL) minced onion

1 garlic clove, chopped

¼ cup (60 mL) olive oil

½ tsp sea salt

½ tsp ground black pepper

3 tbsp red wine vinegar

1 small red chili pepper, seeded and minced

Note: If you don't have a food processor, run a knife through the herbs and garlic until they are finely chopped.

Place all the ingredients in a food processor and pulse until combined. Thin the mixture with additional olive oil, if necessary.

Salsa Verde

This rich herb pesto is perfect with eggs, delicately flavored fish, roast chicken, or as a dressing for boiled potatoes. Substitute chives, arugula, or pungent basil for some of the spinach to vary the flavor.

MAKES I CUP (250 ML)

1 slice white bread, crusts removed

1 garlic clove

1½ tbsp red wine vinegar

1 cup (250 mL) chopped flat leaf parsley

½ cup (125 mL) spinach

2 tbsp capers

½ tsp sea salt

¼ tsp ground black pepper

½ cup (125 mL) fine unfiltered olive oil

I like to use the very best olive oil in dishes that are eaten raw or in recipes in which the oil is an integral part of the dish.

In a food processor, pulse bread and garlic until finely chopped. Add vinegar, parsley, spinach, capers, salt, and pepper, and pulse while adding olive oil until a smooth sauce forms. Add more oil if the mixture is too thick.

Pico de Gallo & Guacamole

I make fresh salsa and guacamole together, because having one without the other is just boring. This is my integrated recipe, optimized for efficiency: Add Pico de Gallo and most of the liquid to mashed avocados and—boom—guacamole. This recipe makes enough for a family of four on taco night, but you can double or triple it for a party.

PICO DE GALLO: MAKES 2 CUPS (500 ML); GUACAMOLE: MAKES 1¼ CUPS (310 ML)

PICO DE GALLO:

1½ cups (375 mL) finely diced tomatoes

4 green onions, chopped

1½ tbsp seeded and minced jalapeño

¼ cup (60 mL) chopped cilantro leaves

2 tbsp lime juice (1 lime)

½ tsp sea salt

GUACAMOLE:

2 ripe avocados

5 tbsp Pico de Gallo

½ tsp sea salt

3 tbsp liquid from Pico de Gallo

PICO DE GALLO:
In a bowl, place all ingredients. Stir to combine. That's it. You're done. Let marinate for 20 minutes before serving.

GUACAMOLE:
Remove flesh from avocados and, in a bowl, mash lightly with a fork. Stir in Pico de Gallo, salt, and liquid from Pico de Gallo. Cover by pressing plastic wrap onto surface of guacamole. Keep covered until ready to serve.

Garden-Style Wor Wonton Soup with Homemade Wontons

I eat wonton soup and crisp vegetables for breakfast more than any other dish, especially in winter. The hot broth infused with spicy ginger soothes and warms. Plus, wonton soup is a great opportunity to get in a serving of vegetables before lunch.

MAKES 4 SERVINGS

4 cups (1 L) low-sodium chicken stock

1 tsp fish sauce

2 ¼-inch (6-mm) slices fresh ginger

2 tbsp kosher salt

16 homemade wontons (p. 33)

1 cup (250 mL) sliced Napa cabbage

4 Shanghai or baby bok choy, quartered lengthwise

1 green onion, chopped

¼ tsp sesame oil

If wontons have been frozen, cook in salted water at a low boil for 5 minutes, then transfer to a pot of simmering stock for another 5 minutes.

In a large pot on high heat, bring 6 qt/L water to a rolling boil.

In a separate pot on medium, heat stock, 2 cups (500 mL) water, fish sauce, and ginger. Bring to a boil, reduce heat to low and simmer.

To 6 qt/L boiling water, add 2 tbsp kosher salt and homemade wontons. Cook for about 3 minutes, then transfer to stock to finish cooking, another 3 minutes. Taste stock and season with salt, if necessary.

Divide cabbage between 4 large soup bowls. Place bok choy in boiling water for 1 minute, remove, and place 4 pieces in each bowl. Place 4 wontons in each bowl and fill with 1½ cups (375 mL) stock. Garnish each bowl with green onions and a drop of sesame oil.

Homemade Wontons

Makes approximately 82 wontons.

Every couple of months my wife and I spend an hour making these wontons, which we freeze on cookie sheets, then bag and keep on hand for a quick meal. A bag of frozen wontons and a tetra-pack of low-sodium chicken stock turns into a nice breakfast or lunch in a matter of minutes. Not complicated, and very tasty.

2 lb (1 kg) ground pork
3 green onions, chopped
3 tbsp grated fresh ginger
½ cup (125 mL) finely chopped
 water chestnuts
2 tsp kosher salt
1 tsp white pepper
1 tbsp sesame oil
1 1 lb (454 g) packet wonton
 wrappers

In a large mixing bowl, combine pork, green onions, ginger, water chestnuts, salt, pepper, and sesame oil and mix thoroughly.

Place a clean, dry tea towel on working surface. Fill a small bowl with tap water. Lay wonton wrapper on tea towel and place 2 tsp filling in middle. Wet edges, fold diagonally, and gently press edges to seal. Repeat until filling is used up. Arrange wontons on a cookie sheet covered by a damp tea towel until ready to cook. Or place tray in freezer for 4 hours before storing wontons in large freezer bags.

Chickpea Salad
with Cilantro Pesto

The mighty chickpea is the solution to many of our most pressing conundrums: What should I eat on Meatless Mondays? How can I better control my cholesterol? What food can reduce my risk of cancer? What is the world's healthiest and most sustainable protein source? My chickpea salad is the delicious answer to all these questions.

MAKES 4–6 SERVINGS

2 cups (500 mL) chickpeas, cooked or canned

½ cup (125 mL) diced yellow bell peppers

½ cup (125 mL) chopped green onions

¾ packed cup (185 mL) chopped fresh cilantro

1 tsp coarse sea salt

⅛ tsp ground black pepper

2 tbsp lime juice

1 garlic clove

2½ tbsp extra virgin olive oil

Rinse chickpeas in cold water and drain. In a large mixing bowl, combine chickpeas, peppers, and onions.

In a food processor, combine cilantro, salt, pepper, lime juice, garlic, and olive oil, and pulse until smooth. Pour cilantro mixture over chickpeas and stir to coat. Let stand 30 minutes.

Herbed Tabbouleh

Tabbouleh is a delicious template for creativity. I use mint and oregano to flavor this version, but if you have dill, cilantro, marjoram, or any tender herb, feel free to substitute—or bring everyone to the party.

MAKES 6 SERVINGS

1 cup (250 mL) medium grain bulgur

2 cups (500 mL) boiling water

1 tsp coarse sea salt

2 tbsp lemon juice

2 tbsp olive oil

¼ tsp ground black pepper

1 packed cup (250 mL) chopped parsley

1 tbsp chopped fresh mint

1 tbsp chopped fresh oregano

4 green onions, chopped

½ cup (125 mL) diced tomatoes

In a large bowl, combine bulgur and boiling water. Cover with a plate and let stand for 30 minutes. Drain and set aside to cool.

In a large bowl, combine salt and lemon juice, and stir until mostly dissolved. Add olive oil and pepper. Stir in bulgur, parsley, mint, oregano, green onions, and tomatoes, and toss to coat.

Radish & White Bean Salad

Crunchy radishes and creamy cannellini beans merge
in a delightful, briny vinaigrette.

2 anchovy fillets

1 tsp Dijon mustard

1 tsp grainy mustard

½ tsp coarse sea salt

2 tbsp white wine or champagne vinegar

3 tbsp unfiltered extra virgin olive oil

¼ cup (60 mL) chopped flat-leaf parsley

¼ cup (60 mL) chopped green onions

1¼ cups (310 mL) cooked cannellini beans

1¼ cups (310 mL) diced radishes

In a large bowl, combine anchovies, Dijon and grainy mustard, and salt. With a wooden spoon, mash until the anchovies form a paste.

Add vinegar and olive oil and stir to combine. Add parsley, green onions, cannellini beans, and radishes and stir to coat. Set aside for 1 hour to marinate before serving.

Quick Pickled Shallot Dressing

The shallot in this dressing is raw, but the natural pungency and heat are mellowed with a simple brine, using salt and lemon juice.

MAKES ¼ CUP (60 ML)

1 shallot, peeled and minced

1 tsp coarse sea salt

2 tbsp lemon juice

¼ tsp ground black pepper

3 tbsp extra virgin olive oil

1 tbsp minced fresh oregano

1 tsp Dijon mustard

In a small bowl, mash shallots and salt with your fingertips. Add lemon juice and pepper and set aside for 15 minutes. Add olive oil, oregano, and mustard. Pour dressing into a small jar and seal with a lid. Shake briskly just before serving.

Goddess of the Ranch Dressing

Fresh tarragon, parsley, and dill provide herbaceous punch to this Green Goddess/Ranch dressing hybrid. Serve over fresh greens or as a dip for crudités.

MAKES 1 CUP (250 ML)

½ cup (125 mL) olive oil mayonnaise

2 tbsp buttermilk

½ tsp mustard powder

1 garlic clove, minced

2 green onions, chopped

¼ cup (60 mL) chopped flat-leaf parsley

1½ tbsp chopped fresh dill

1 tbsp chopped fresh tarragon

½ tsp kosher salt

½ tsp ground black pepper

1 anchovy fillet

In a food processor, blend all ingredients until smooth, about 1 minute.

Chicken & Rainbow Chard

I first created this recipe after a helpful deer came and ate all the leaves off my chard plants one spring. I used the remaining white, yellow, red, and green stalks to make supper that night. Since then, it's become something of a favorite.

MAKES 6 SERVINGS

1 3–4 lb (1.4–1.8 kg) chicken, cut into pieces

1 tsp kosher salt

½ tsp ground black pepper

¼ cup (60 mL) extra virgin olive oil

2 garlic cloves, sliced

1 dried red chili pepper, crumbled

2 cups (500 mL) diced chard stalks

2 lb (1 kg) plum tomatoes, chopped

1 cup (250 mL) chopped chard leaves

2 tbsp kosher salt

1 lb (500 g) dried linguini

½ cup (250 mL) grated Pecorino cheese

¼ cup (125 mL) chopped flat-leaf parsley or basil

Don't crowd the pan when searing meat or moisture will build up and prevent it from browning, which builds depth of flavor.

In the off-season, substitute 1 28-oz (794-g) can of diced tomatoes for 2 lb (2 kg) fresh tomatoes.

Season chicken on all sides with salt and pepper. In a large, flat-bottomed pan on medium, heat oil. Add chicken and brown on both sides. Remove chicken pieces, set aside, and add garlic, chili, and chard stalks. Sauté to soften, about 3 minutes, then add tomatoes. When tomatoes start to break down into sauce, return chicken to pan with chard leaves. Cover pan with a lid and let simmer for 30 minutes. Remove chicken pieces and set aside again.

In a large pot on high heat, bring 6 qt/L water to a boil. Add salt and linguini, and cook for 6 minutes. Drain, add pasta to sauce, and simmer for 5 minutes. Top with chicken pieces. Sprinkle with cheese and parsley.

Chicken Fricassee with Garden Vegetables

Fricassee is a dish you can make at any time of year, but it is truly at its best when you have leeks, baby carrots, and peas from the garden. (Diced carrots and frozen peas are just fine the rest of the year.) Because this dish is cooked on the bone, every bit of chicken flavor comes through. It's a perfect way to prepare a pasture-raised chicken; the long simmering time ensures tender meat. Serve with Frank Shore's Dumplings (p. 164) or Cheddar Dill Biscuits (p. 163).

MAKES 4–6 SERVINGS

- 2 tbsp extra virgin olive oil, divided
- 1 3–4 lb (1.4–1.8 kg) chicken, cut into pieces (or 2½ lb [1 kg] bone-in, skin-on chicken breasts)
- 2 tsp kosher salt, divided
- 1 tsp ground black pepper, divided
- 4 cups (1 L) low-sodium chicken stock or water
- 4 bay leaves
- 1 cup (250 mL) diced celery
- 2 cups (500 mL) baby carrots
- 1 cup (250 mL) minced leeks (white part only; reserve greens for stock)
- ½ cup (125 mL) cream
- ¼ cup (60 mL) all-purpose flour
- ½ cup (125 mL) chopped flat-leaf parsley
- 1 cup (250 mL) peas

Pasture-raised animals live a more natural life and eat a more natural diet than those raised in an industrial setting. The resulting meat also has a fat profile that is more nutritious for human beings. Win-win.

In a large flat-bottomed pan on medium, heat 1 tbsp olive oil. Season chicken pieces on all sides with 1 tsp salt and pepper. Place skin-side down in pan. Fry chicken in batches to avoid crowding. Try not to move chicken for at least 4 minutes, when it will naturally release from pan without sticking. Fry chicken until golden brown, about 5–6 minutes. Turn pieces and brown for another 5 minutes. Add stock, bay leaves, and any trimmings from celery and carrots, dark green tops of leeks, and parsley stems. Bring to a boil, then reduce heat and simmer twenty minutes. Turn chicken over and simmer for another 20 minutes. Remove chicken, discard skin, and set aside. Strain cooking broth into a large bowl and set aside. Discard vegetable trimmings.

Place pan on medium heat and add 1 tbsp olive oil, celery, carrots, and leeks, and sauté until softened. Add 3 cups (750 mL) cooking broth and bring to a simmer. Whisk cream and flour together until smooth and add to pan, stirring constantly with whisk to incorporate and eliminate lumps. Simmer until thickened, about 5 minutes. Add remaining salt and pepper to taste.

Remove chicken meat from bones, shred into bite-sized pieces, and return to pan. Simmer gently for 10 minutes. Stir in parsley and peas. Thin with remaining stock, if necessary.

Use white part of leeks in fricassee, but save dark green leek tops, along with carrot trimmings, parsley stems, and bottoms of celery stalks to use in cooking liquid.

Cheddar Dill Biscuits (p. 163)

Broiled Sockeye with Garden Herbs

Wild-caught sockeye salmon is certified sustainable by SeaChoice, Ocean Wise, and the Marine Stewardship Council (see p. 89). While there are some concerns about spawning returns and habitat degradation, Pacific sockeye is one of the world's most intensively managed and studied fisheries. For now, it remains a better choice than Atlantic salmon farmed in net pens.

MAKES 4 SERVINGS

1 sockeye fillet, pin bones removed	1 tbsp extra virgin olive oil
⅛ tsp kosher salt	2 tsp Dijon mustard
⅛ tsp ground black pepper	2 tsp grainy mustard
1 garlic clove, minced	½ tbsp finely chopped fresh rosemary
1 tsp white wine	1 tsp fresh thyme leaves

To remove pin bones from salmon fillet: Lay salmon skin-side down and run your fingertips along thickest part of fillet to find tips of pin bones. Use a pair of clean needle-nose pliers to grasp end of each bone; pull gently in direction bones point, usually a 45° angle toward thick end of the fillet. I keep a set of pliers around strictly for kitchen jobs.

Preheat broiler to high. Place salmon skin-side down on a cookie sheet lined with foil. (You can thank me for that tip later.) Season salmon with salt and pepper. Mash garlic to a paste using flat side of a knife.

In a small mixing bowl, combine garlic, wine, olive oil, and Dijon and grainy mustard.

Broil salmon on middle rack for 5 minutes. Remove from oven. Apply garlic mixture evenly over fish, sprinkle with rosemary and thyme, and broil salmon until thickest part of fillet is firm to the touch, about 5–10 minutes.

To add another dimension of flavor, place salmon on a soaked cedar plank and bake on high heat on your outdoor barbecue grill with the lid down until firm to the touch.

Clockwise from top right: Rice Pilaf (p. 55), Broilded Sockeye with Garden Herbs (opposite), Radish & White Bean Salad (p. 36)

Garden Variety Lettuce Wraps

Kids love food they can build at the table. (I do, too!) Lettuce wraps are traditionally made with ground pork, which can contain as much as twenty percent fat. Lower the fat by using lean ground turkey instead.

MAKES 4 SERVINGS

1 tbsp canola oil

1 lb (500 g) ground pork or turkey

1 tbsp grated ginger

1 8-oz (227-g) tin water chestnuts, finely chopped

½ cup (125 mL) grated carrot

1 8-oz (227-g) tin bamboo shoots, finely diced

½ cup (125 mL) chopped green onions

2 tbsp oyster sauce

1 tsp sesame oil

2 tbsp light soy sauce

2 tsp cornstarch

1 tbsp Chinese rice wine or sherry

5 oz (150 g) crispy dried chow mein noodles

1 cup (250 mL) bean sprouts

12 iceberg lettuce leaves

Lettuce wraps are traditionally made with iceberg lettuce leaves, but I often have an oversupply of chard. Perhaps you do, too. If you feel adventurous, try substituting chard leaves blanched in boiling water for 30 seconds.

In a large wok on high, heat oil and swirl to coat. Add pork and stir-fry, breaking up meat until cooked through. Stir in ginger, water chestnuts, carrots, bamboo shoots, and green onions.

In a small bowl, combine oyster sauce, sesame oil, and soy sauce. Pour over meat mixture in pan. In a separate bowl, whisk cornstarch and rice wine, then pour over meat mixture. Stir gently until sauce thickens. Remove from heat and stir in chow mein noodles and bean sprouts.

To serve, place ¼–½ cup (60–125 mL) meat filling on each lettuce leaf. Roll half leaf over mixture, fold sides in, and fold remaining flap over top.

Veal Scallopini with Parsley Caper Sauce

The sauce for this dish is made the minute the meat leaves the pan, adding flavor, freshness, and luxurious richness—a simple but effective French technique. You can find veal scallopini at any good Italian butcher shop. Ask your butcher to run it through "the machine," a device that makes small slices through the cutlet for added tenderness. He will nod and smile at your insider knowledge. For those of you who avoid eating veal, substitute chicken breasts pounded thin and fried for an extra minute, so it's cooked through. Serve this with Parsley Butter Noodles (p. 59).

MAKES 4 SERVINGS

1 tsp kosher salt

½ tsp pepper

4 veal cutlets, ¼-in (6-mm) thick

1 cup (250 mL) all-purpose flour

2–3 tbsp extra virgin olive oil

2 tbsp white wine

½ cup (125 mL) low-sodium chicken stock

2 tbsp capers

2 tbsp lemon juice

2 tbsp butter

½ cup (125 mL) chopped parsley leaves

Combine salt and pepper and use half mixture to season veal on both sides. Combine remainder of salt and pepper with flour and dredge veal.

In a large sauté pan on medium-high, heat 2 tbsp olive oil. Fry cutlets quickly, about 1 minute a side, until lightly browned. Remove from pan and set veal aside. Add more oil to pan, if necessary, then add 1 tbsp dredging flour and heat until fragrant, about 1 minute. Remove from heat and whisk in wine and stock. Return pan to heat and whisk until sauce thickens. Stir in capers and lemon juice. Taste sauce and season with salt and pepper, if desired. Stir in butter until melted. Add parsley. Pour sauce over veal and serve immediately.

The Green Man's Meatloaf

I love meatloaf so much that every time my wife goes out of town, I try to live on it. Even people who don't like meatloaf (trust me, they are out there) will like this one. If you haven't made my catsup, just use store-bought. I won't say anything.

MAKES 6 SERVINGS

1 lb (500 g) lean ground beef

1 lb (500 g) ground pork

1 cup (250 mL) bread crumbs

2 cups (500 mL) chopped fresh spinach

2 tbsp chopped fresh flat-leaf parsley

2 tbsp chopped fresh basil

2 large eggs

¼ cup (60 mL) beef or chicken stock

¼ cup (60 mL) Fresh Tomato Catsup (p. 120)

1 plum-sized tomato, minced

1 tsp kosher salt

2 tsp Louisiana-style hot sauce

1 tsp Worcestershire sauce

Some people like a glaze on meat loaf. If you are one of these people, simply brush the outside of the loaf with Fresh Tomato Catsup halfway through the cooking process.

Preheat oven to 350°F (180°C).

Place beef, pork, bread crumbs, spinach, parsley, and basil in a large bowl and mix lightly, breaking up meat with your fingers. In a separate bowl, combine eggs, stock, catsup, tomato, salt, hot sauce, and Worcestershire sauce. Pour wet ingredients over meat mixture and combine well.

Line a baking sheet with foil and form a loaf about 12 x 5 in (30.5 x 13 cm). Refrigerate for 1 hour.

Bake for 1 hour and 15 minutes or until internal temperature reaches 165°F (75°C). Let stand for 5 minutes before serving in thick slices.

Kangaroo Meatballs in Roasted Red Pepper Sauce

Kangaroo is available in North America from specialty butcher shops and game meat suppliers. If you worry about the impact that industrial meat production has on the planet, kangaroo might be the answer to your concerns. It has a taste not unlike mild venison and a healthier omega-3 to omega-6 fatty acid ratio than beef. If you know a hunter, ground elk or venison is a good substitute where kangaroo isn't available. Serve with rice or pasta, or as an appetizer platter that will keep the conversation hopping.

MAKES 4 SERVINGS

ROASTED RED PEPPERS:

4 red bell peppers

ROASTED RED PEPPER SAUCE:

1 tbsp olive oil

1 garlic clove, minced

½ cup (125 mL) diced onions

2 roasted red bell peppers

3 cups (750 mL) diced tomatoes

1 tsp coarse sea salt

½ tsp ground black pepper

If you are pressed for time, use store-bought roasted red peppers to speed things up.

ROASTED RED PEPPERS

With a gas stove: Turn flame to high and place an entire red pepper on burner. Turn with tongs once per minute until skin has blackened. Under a broiler: Preheat broiler to high. Place peppers on a baking sheet on highest rack of oven. As skin blackens, turn peppers with tongs.

When peppers are blackened over most of their surface, place them in a paper bag and close to seal. Wait 10 minutes while peppers soften and cool. Remove from bag and loosen skin with fingertips to remove. Split pepper with a knife and remove stem and seeds.

ROASTED RED PEPPER SAUCE

In a large saucepan on medium, heat olive oil. Sauté garlic and onions until soft, about 3 minutes. Dice roasted red peppers and add to saucepan. Add tomatoes, salt, and pepper and simmer until tomatoes sweeten. (Just taste it every 15 minutes or so; you'll know when you're there.)

In a food processor, pulse mixture 1 cup (250 mL) at a time. Set aside.

ROO BALLS:

1 lb (500 g) ground kangaroo

¼ cup (60 mL) fine bread crumbs

¼ cup (60 mL) minced onions

1 garlic clove, minced

1 large egg

1 tsp kosher salt

½ tsp ground black pepper

½ tsp dried oregano

½ tsp dried thyme

½ cup (125 mL) chopped fresh parsley

1 tbsp water

1–2 tbsp olive oil

In a large mixing bowl, crumble meat with your fingers. Add remainder of ingredients except olive oil and knead until well combined. Form into 1-in (2.5-cm) balls.

In a large cast-iron frying pan on medium-high, heat olive oil. Sear meatballs on all sides. Add Roasted Red Pepper Sauce and simmer for 20 minutes.

Italian Sausage Meatballs

Sausage meatballs are very tasty when simmered in Arrabiata Sauce (p. 156) and served over pasta. Make them ahead of time and freeze, then cook them for an easy weeknight meal or chop them up as a topping for pizza (p. 194).

MAKES 12 MEATBALLS

1 lb (500 g) ground pork shoulder

1 tbsp fennel seeds, crushed

1 tbsp hot paprika

2 tbsp red wine

¼ tsp ground black pepper

⅛ tsp ground nutmeg

2 tsp kosher salt

1 garlic clove, minced

1 tbsp fresh oregano leaves

2 tbsp olive oil, for frying

With whole spices such as fennel seeds in this recipe, you measure first, then crush. If you do it the other way, you have to guess how much whole spice will make the right amount crushed.

In a large bowl, combine pork, fennel seeds, paprika, red wine, pepper, nutmeg, salt, garlic, and oregano. Mix vigorously with hands or a large spoon for about 1 minute.

To make meatballs, roll 2 tbsp meat mixture between your palms to form a ball. In a frying pan on medium, heat olive oil. Fry meatballs in batches until browned and firm to the touch.

Saag Paneer

When I go looking for ways to use garden greens, I often turn to Indian cuisine. Saag paneer is creamed spinach with crispy, fried paneer, a home-style Indian cheese with a texture like extra-firm tofu—so, for a vegan meal, you can easily substitute tofu. And don't get stuck on using only spinach for this dish; any tender greens from the garden will work. Consider turnip greens, kale, beet tops, or chard to replace some or all of the spinach. I like to mix it up. Serve with Rice Pilaf (p. 55) or Super Simple Pita Bread (p. 62).

MAKES 4 SERVINGS

1 lb (500 g) spinach

½ lb (250 g) paneer

2 tbsp canola oil

¾ cup (185 mL) minced leeks, white and
pale green parts only

2 tsp ground coriander

2 tsp ground cumin

1 tsp black mustard seeds

¼ tsp cayenne pepper

1½ tsp kosher salt

½ cup (125 mL) yogurt

Fill a kettle with 2 qt/L water and bring to a boil. In a large mixing bowl, add spinach and pour boiling water over top. Let stand for 3 minutes, then drain. In a food processor, purée spinach.

Cut paneer into ¾-in (2-cm) cubes. In a large non-stick frying pan on medium, heat oil. Add paneer and fry until browned on three sides.

Remove paneer and set aside. To frying pan, add leeks and sauté until golden, about 3 minutes. Add coriander, cumin, and mustard seeds, and stir for 1 minute. Add spinach, cayenne, salt, and ½ cup (125 mL) water. Bring to a boil, then reduce heat to low and simmer for 20 minutes. Remove from heat and stir in yogurt. Return paneer to pan and coat with spinach mixture.

Sautéed Chard & Onions

I know chard isn't the most popular vegetable. In the social hierarchy of the supermarket, broccoli and carrots are quarterbacking the football team and captaining the cheerleading squad, and romaine lettuce is that Mexican exchange student that everyone seems to like more than they like you. High school sucks, but chard doesn't have to.

MAKES 4 SERVINGS

2 tbsp olive oil

½ cup (125 mL) diced onions

½ tsp sea salt

4 garlic cloves, minced

1 bunch rainbow chard, about 6 large stalks

1 tbsp red wine vinegar

salt and ground black pepper, to taste

Chard grows vigorously in the garden, producing tender stalks and large, dark green leaves. Chard can also be grown successfully in 2- or 3-gallon pots well into the fall.

Mulch chard with 6 in (15 cm) of brown leaves or compost before the first hard frost of the winter, and there's a good chance it will come back in early spring, long before it's safe to plant seeds for any other crop.

In a flat-bottomed pan on medium, heat olive oil. Add onions and salt, and sauté until soft, about 5 minutes. Add garlic and sauté for another minute. Separate chard stalks from leaves and dice.

Add chard stalks to pan and sauté for 2 minutes. Cut chard leaves into 1 in (2.5 cm) strips and add to pan with vinegar, turning until wilted. Taste and season with salt and pepper, if desired.

Sicilian Chard

Depending on where you live, overwintering chard is likely to be the first vegetable to achieve prodigious production when spring arrives. When it does, this is a delicious and simple way to prepare it.

MAKES 6 SERVINGS

1 tbsp olive oil

1 garlic clove, thinly sliced

½ tsp crushed chili flakes

2 cups (500 mL) diced chard stalks

1 tsp coarse sea salt

4 cups (1 L) chopped chard leaves

1 tbsp lemon juice

1 tbsp unfiltered extra virgin olive oil

In a large flat-bottomed pan on medium, heat olive oil. Add garlic and chilies, stirring for 1 minute. Add chard stalks and salt and sauté until softened, about 3 minutes. Add chard leaves and sauté for 3 minutes to wilt and reduce moisture.

Transfer mixture to a serving dish and drizzle with lemon juice and olive oil.

Wild Rice & Greens

My wife Darcy came up with this dish, loaded with fiber and antioxidants, as a healthy vegetarian meal for two. Experiment with different mushrooms and leafy greens to change it up.

MAKES 2 SERVINGS (OR 4 AS A SIDE)

1 shallot, minced

2 tbsp butter

1 cup (250 mL) sliced white mushrooms

½ tsp kosher salt

¼ tsp ground black pepper

1 cup (250 mL) mixed brown and wild rice

1¾ cups low-sodium chicken stock or water

1½ cups (375 mL) chopped lacinato kale

¼ cup (60 mL) sunflower seeds (optional)

Commercial stocks are often seasoned with salt. When making a recipe that calls for both stock and salt, hold back on adding some or all of the salt until you're sure the dish needs it.

In a pot on medium-low heat, sauté shallots in butter for 2 minutes. Add mushrooms, salt, and pepper and sauté for 3 minutes. Add rice and stir to coat with butter, then add stock and kale. Taste cooking liquid and season with salt, if desired. Increase heat to high and bring to a boil for 2 minutes.

Cover with a lid, reduce heat to low, and cook for 50 minutes. Loosen rice with a fork, replace lid, turn off heat, and leave pot on burner for 15 minutes. Top with sunflower seeds and serve.

Rice Pilaf

A colorful side dish for Red Lentil Dal (p. 58) or Broiled Salmon (p. 42).
Choose a saucepan with a tight-fitting lid.

A colorful side dish for Red Lentil Dal (p. 58) or Broiled Salmon (p. 42).

MAKES 4 SERVINGS

2 tbsp olive oil

¼ cup (60 mL) minced shallot

1 garlic clove, minced

½ cup (125 mL) finely diced carrot

1 cup (250 mL) basmati rice

½ tsp turmeric

1½ cups (375 mL) low-sodium stock

1 tsp kosher salt

½ cup (125 mL) fresh peas

¼ cup (60 mL) slivered almonds

In a saucepan on medium, heat oil. Add shallots and sauté until soft, about 3 minutes. Add garlic and carrots, and stir for 1 minute. Add rice (dry, don't rinse it), and stir until coated in oil. Add turmeric, stock, and salt, and bring to a boil. Reduce heat to low. Cover with lid and cook for 10 minutes.

Turn heat off, leaving pot covered on burner for another 10 minutes. Stir in peas and let sit for 5 minutes. Top with slivered almonds.

Spicy Broccoli Rabe with Pasta

Some vegetables are meant for grown-up taste buds, and broccoli rabe may be top of the list. Also known as rapini, this slightly bitter green, related to turnips, hates growing in the heat, preferring the cool soils of spring and autumn. This dish stands up as a meal on its own or as a side that incorporates starch and a green vegetable in one. You can also substitute broccoli or gai lan, whichever is looking good in the garden that day.

MAKES 4–6 SERVINGS

2 tbsp kosher salt, for pasta water

⅓ cup (80 mL) walnut halves

1 tbsp extra virgin olive oil

5 strips bacon, cut into ¼-in (6-mm) strips

1 medium onion, halved and thinly sliced

1 garlic clove, minced

1 tsp fennel seeds, crushed

1 dried red chili pepper, crumbled

1 lb (500 g) broccoli rabe

1 lb (500 g) dried farfalle (bow-tie pasta)

½ cup (125 mL) grated Parmesan cheese

Broccoli's sweet secret: When you harvest broccoli, cut off plenty of stem with the main floret. For this dish, if you use broccoli instead of rabe, use both florets and heart of broccoli stem. Use a knife to cut away the tough skin on the outside of the stem to reveal the sweetest and most tender part of the plant.

In a large pot on high heat, bring 6 qt/L water and salt to a boil.

In a sauté pan on medium heat, toast walnuts for about 2 minutes, stirring frequently to prevent burning. Remove walnuts from pan, crumble with your fingers, and set aside. In same pan, warm olive oil. Add bacon and fry until crispy. Add onions, garlic, fennel seeds, and chili. Cook until onions are lightly browned. Cut broccoli rabe into 2-in (5-cm) pieces; separate thick stems from slender tops and leaves. Add broccoli rabe stems to pan and cook for 2 minutes, then add leaves. Reduce heat to low.

Add pasta to boiling water and cook al dente, according to package directions. Drain pasta, reserving 1 cup (250 mL) water. Add pasta, cheese, and a little reserved pasta water to pan and toss gently to combine. Add more water, a little at a time, to form a creamy sauce. Garnish each serving with toasted walnuts.

Red Lentil Dal

Dal is a soup or stew made from lentils that's served in virtually every corner of India. Lentils are high in fiber and protein—and a perfect choice if you are cutting back on meat for the sake of the planet or your own health. I collect coriander seeds from my overgrown cilantro plants and top the dish with fresh cilantro leaves from the younger plants. Serve with Rice Pilaf (p. 55).

MAKES 4 SERVINGS

1 cup (250 mL) red lentils

2 plum tomatoes, chopped

¼ tsp ground turmeric

1½ tsp ground cumin

1 tsp ground coriander

½ tsp kosher salt

2 green chili peppers, minced

3 tbsp canola oil

3 garlic cloves, minced

1 cup (250 mL) diced onions

2 tbsp chopped cilantro leaves

Rinse lentils thoroughly in cold water and drain. In a saucepan on high heat, bring lentils to a boil in 2¼ cups (530 mL) water. Remove surface scum with a spoon. Add tomatoes, turmeric, cumin, and coriander, and bring to a boil again. Reduce heat and simmer for 40 minutes. Add salt and chilies and simmer for another 10 minutes.

In a frying pan on medium, heat oil. Sauté garlic and onions until golden brown, about 5 minutes. Combine lentil and onion mixtures and top with cilantro.

Parsley Butter Noodles

I wrestled with myself over whether to include this recipe, and then I wrestled with myself over whether it really is even a recipe. Despite its simplicity, I really like the combination of ingredients—and I never pass up the opportunity to add more green to a plate. Serve as a side with Veal Scallopini (p. 46).

MAKES 4 SERVINGS

12 oz (340 g) dried egg noodles

¼ cup (60 mL) salted butter

2 tbsp olive oil

½ cup (125 mL) chopped flat-leaf parsley

In a large pot on high heat, cook noodles in 6 qt/L water, according to package directions. Drain and return to pot. Add butter, olive oil, and parsley and cover with a lid for 2 minutes. Stir and serve immediately.

The Original Rhubarb-Blueberry Crumble

Old recipes can be a challenge. I have binders full of hand-written recipes on yellowed paper, with no oven temperature or directions. Some list ingredients without amounts. If you were going to cook back in the day, it was just assumed that you learned the recipe from Mom or Nana. In the time-honored tradition of my ancestors, I present to you a crumble the way Nana used to do it, but I've given you measured amounts and an oven temperature for your convenience.
Serve hot with a big scoop of vanilla ice cream.

MAKES 6–8 SERVINGS

TOPPING:

½ cup (125 mL) salted butter

1 cup (250 mL) rolled oats

½ cup (125 mL) all-purpose flour

¾ cup (185 mL) brown sugar

½ cup (125 mL) chopped walnuts and
   pecans

½ tsp ground cinnamon

FILLING:

6 cups (1.5 L) diced rhubarb

2 cups (500 mL) blueberries or blackberries

¼ cup (60 mL) white sugar

1 tbsp grated fresh ginger

2 tbsp cornstarch

Preheat oven to 350°F (180°C).

In a large bowl, add all topping ingredients. Combine well with your hands to form a ball, then set aside.

In a large (8 x 11.5 x 2-in [20 x 29 x 5-cm]) baking dish, combine all filling ingredients. Stir until combined. Crumble topping mixture over filling and bake until fruit is bubbling and topping browned, about 45 minutes.

Super Simple Pita Bread

I get that people are afraid to make bread. Baking is chemistry—get one component wrong or do something in the wrong order, and disaster is yours to wear like an albatross. Pita is the exception: the recipe is short, the technique simple, and the result assured. Serve with Lamb & Spinach Kebabs (p. 144) or Saag Paneer (p. 51).

MAKES 8 PITAS

1 tbsp fast-acting yeast

2½ cups (625 mL) warm water

3 cups (750 mL) bread flour

1½ tsp kosher salt

2 tbsp olive oil, divided

1½ cups (375 mL) all-purpose flour

1 cup (250 mL) whole wheat flour

Pita dough has to rise twice for 1 hour each time, which gives you plenty of time to have a glass of wine or two.

You can also grill pita on a hot barbecue. Preheat to high and grill for about 1 minute on each side with the lid down, until pitas are puffy and steaming.

In a large mixing bowl, combine yeast and water. Add bread flour 1 cup (250 mL) at a time, using a spoon to incorporate flour and liquid. Stir for 1 minute, until smooth. Cover bowl with beeswax wrap or cling film and set in a warm location for 1 hour.

Add salt and 1 tbsp olive oil to mixture and stir in all-purpose and whole wheat flour until dough forms. Coat working surface with all-purpose flour and turn dough out. Knead until dough is smooth and elastic, adding more flour as required. Coat inside of a separate bowl with remaining olive oil and place dough inside. Cover and place in a warm location until it doubles in size, about 1 hour.

Place a baking sheet or pizza stone in middle of oven and preheat to 500°F (260°C). Cut dough into 8 pieces. Form each piece into a ball and place on a floured surface. Roll each into a circle about 8 in (2 cm) across. Bake for about 3 minutes, until puffy and just browned.

Summer

A Season of Edible Delights

The growing season is a parade of delicious firsts. Rhubarb emerges after the ground thaws, followed quickly by peas and broad beans. I can't wait to collect a cup of fresh peas to mash with Parmesan and olive oil, a delirious moment that comes but once a year. The first basil begets the first fresh pesto. Then come new potatoes and baby carrots, often in quantities that threaten to overwhelm the kitchen and the cook.

Each new crop is an occasion for celebration and reflection. There is nothing instant about growing your own food, but the gratification is very real. The earth's rhythms are decidedly languid compared to the pace of urban life. Strawberries arrive on their own schedule, and they don't stay long, so when I eat one in the garden, I often find myself sitting down to feel the sun on my face. I don't really even cultivate strawberries; they grow voluntarily from the cracks between the rocks in my retaining wall, as if to reward me for taking a few minutes to visit the garden.

With food gardening, time is reckoned in seasons, rather than in instant updates and smartphone alert chimes. It lowers my blood pressure to run the hose over the morning's radish harvest; it grounds me to share with my neighbors whatever is in abundance that day. It is particularly satisfying to sit down to a family meal of foods that I have grown myself and picked at the peak of freshness when their nutritional value is highest. By sourcing vegetables from the garden or from my local farmers market I feel secure that no pesticides or other chemicals have come in contact with my food.

In summer, the garden really is your fridge and your grocery store. You needn't burn any gas to pick up food for dinner when it grows on the balcony, under the kitchen window, and all over the backyard. Go shopping in the fresh air, and while you're out there, stop and eat a strawberry or a handful of peas.

TOUGHEN UP YOUR TRANSPLANTS

Being transplanted into the garden is a traumatic experience for a seedling. After spending anywhere from four to twelve weeks on a warm windowsill or in a commercial-grade greenhouse at your local nursery, tender young plants are vulnerable to extremes of temperature and even to direct sunlight. The greenhouse environment may be bright, but it does not allow the intense radiation of direct sunlight to penetrate. Sunburn can damage or even kill a young plant.

Place a tall pail or an empty planter 1 in (2.5 cm) to the south of new transplants to provide temporary shade at midday.

Seedlings should be carefully hardened off in the yard before being transplanted to ensure they are equipped to survive low overnight temperatures in early spring or full sun if you are transplanting during the summer. For their first night outside, choose a location that is sheltered and close to the house, where it is usually a few degrees warmer than the rest of the yard. During hot summer weather, protect the seedlings from the sun at midday, but make sure they get some direct sun in the morning and late afternoon. Continue this process for three to seven days.

Seedlings transplanted into the garden in

early spring should be protected if there is any danger of frost. A simple cloche made from a 4-qt/L milk jug with the bottom and cap removed can be placed over seedlings if the weather turns unexpectedly cold. The cloche will also gain heat from the sun during the day, which speeds growth.

In hot summer weather, transplant late in the day. The move from pot to garden soil is a shock, and your seedlings will need all night and more to recover. Even sun-lovers such as tomatoes are easily damaged right after transplanting. For large plants such as tomato vines, cauliflower, broccoli, and kale, add ½ cup (125 mL) Basic Fertilizer Mix (p. 14) to the soil with well-rotted compost, and "mud" the root ball in with plenty of water.

In hot, sunny weather, transplanted lettuce seedlings should be protected from midday sun for at least a week. Plant lettuces to the north and east of taller plants to take advantage of the shade they provide during the hottest part of the day.

COMPANION PLANTING AND NATURAL SUCCESSION

Companion planting is a popular theme in garden lore. Organic gardeners put certain plants together to protect vulnerable crops from predators ranging from deer to beetles. Or—less believably—to enhance the flavors of certain vegetables, such as basil's supposedly magical influence on the flavor of tomatoes. Most of the widely recognized tenets of companion planting remain very much in the realm of folk wisdom, though, as there is little credible science to back their claims.

You can, however, use a form of companion planting—what I call succession planting—to increase the productivity of some of your garden beds. Here are a few tricks that I use:

Grow fast and slow, together: Sow radishes and carrots together in spring, alternating seeds about an inch apart in rows 6 in (15 cm) apart. That's half the normal row spacing. The radishes will mature and be harvested within five weeks, about the time that slower-growing carrots begin to bulk up. Radishes take little in the way of nutrients from the soil and the carrots benefit from the extra space at this stage. Harvest baby carrots at the beginning of summer, and begin to introduce broccoli or cauliflower seedlings in the newly available space.

Grow plants that nourish one another: Plant spinach seeds among maturing pea vines. Peas collect nitrogen from the atmosphere and store it in nodules on their root system. Spinach is a heavy nitrogen feeder. When you harvest peas, cut the vines off at the soil, leaving the roots—and the nitrogen—in place.

Make mini-microclimates: Plant zucchini seedlings 3 ft (1 m) apart and sprinkle a few arugula seeds in between, covering them lightly. The shade from the zucchini leaves will help the cool-weather arugula thrive in the summer heat.

Combine early-, middle-, and late-season vegetables: Sow mesclun greens such as mizuna, corn salad, and radicchio in spring. Just sprinkle the seeds around the bed and rake them in lightly. As you harvest tender young greens in late spring, plant chard seeds into the spaces left by the departing mescluns. By early summer, the greens will have run their course, and you can plant Napa cabbage and collards in

the remaining spaces. The Napa cabbage will be ready to harvest in September, leaving space for the expanding wingspan of the collards. Harvest collard leaves from the bottom of the plant throughout the winter, where the climate allows it.

HOW TO GROW TOMATOES

Tomatoes thrive through long, hot, dry summers. A good growing season can deliver hundreds of tomatoes from a modest number of vines, especially inland. Near the coast, it's more hit and miss. Tomato vines are reasonably resistant to cold in late spring, but quickly succumb to blight if the weather turns wet at the end of summer. Crowding tomatoes reduces air circulation and promotes blight, so plant your vines 3 ft (1 m) apart. (If you do get hit with blight, don't put the vines in your compost. Remove them from the property.)

To extend your harvest, choose a mix of early- and late-bearing varieties and a selection of sauce tomatoes (Amish Paste, Roma, San Marzano) and eating tomatoes (Black Krim, Stupice, Prudens Purple, Black Cherry, Gold Nugget).

Potted tomatoes will grow comfortably in five-gallon containers. Use clean soil from the garden center and blend with 1 cup (250 mL) Basic Fertilizer Mix (p. 14). When the first fruit appears, feed the vines with high-phosphorus liquid fertilizer, such as a blooming formula.

To protect them from drying out, plant tomato vines deeply, so that the lower leaf stems are at the soil's surface. Trim away the bottom leaves and mud the root ball in with plenty of water.

Choose a sunny location in the garden, preferably near a south-facing wall or fence, to plant tomato seedlings. Reflected heat is a real bonus, especially late in the growing season, when it promotes ripening.

Potted or in the garden, tomatoes need support to stay off the ground. Use the strongest stakes you can find, and tie the vines about every 12 in (30.5 cm) with cotton twine. Some people I know use rebar to stake, which used to sound a bit crazy to me. That is, until my one-by-two wooden stakes started snapping like twigs one summer under the weight of the fruit.

Most home garden tomatoes are indeterminate, meaning they keep growing as long as conditions of sun, moisture, and nutrition are favorable. The fast-spreading vines are also their own worst enemy, sprouting new vines called "suckers" that literally suck the life out of the plant, using up nutrients that could be setting fruit.

When the first flower buds appear on your vine, cut or break off all the sucker vines below the flowers. The suckers grow upwards from the junctions where leaf stems attach to the main stem. If you leave the suckers long enough, they will create an impenetrable jungle of foliage and you won't get much fruit. Check your vines at least weekly for new suckers and break them off.

People swear that planting basil with tomatoes protects them from harmful insects. Maybe, maybe not. I do know that whenever I pick a tomato I immediately look for basil because they go together in so many outstanding dishes, so planting them together makes sense. Basil also thrives on the warm, moist, sheltered growing conditions favored by tomatoes, so it's a good match in that sense, too.

HOW TO GROW ASPARAGUS

When you decide to grow asparagus, you are making a multi-year commitment. Your asparagus ferns are going to be a fixture in the garden for up to twenty years, and you will care for young ferns for at least twenty months before you eat your first spear. Don't worry, it's not difficult—and fresh asparagus is so worth it.

There are two paths you can take on your quest for asparagus: You can buy crowns—expensive little pre-grown root systems—or plant from seed. I've done both and found seeds produce healthy asparagus plants just as fast as crowns for one-tenth the price. Consult a good regional seed supplier to obtain an asparagus variety well-suited to local growing conditions. The seeds need consistent moisture and warm soil to germinate, so wait until June to plant. (If you have a greenhouse or solarium, you can start two months earlier.)

In late spring, fill ten 4-inch pots with sterile potting mix and plant three to four seeds per pot. Place the pots in a warm, sheltered location, and be prepared to wait at least one month to see sprouts. Keep them watered throughout the summer. By mid-September, you should have ten spindly, foot-high (30.5-cm) ferns to transplant.

Location is important to asparagus. They won't be moving, at least not for the next decade, so make sure you get the soil in really good shape. Pick a sunny, well-drained location.

Waterlogged roots will die; deep sandy soil on higher ground is preferable. Dig the soil deeply and mix in well-composted manure and 1 cup (250 mL) Basic Fertilizer Mix (p. 14) for each pot of seedlings.

Plant the seedlings so that the root balls are 6 in (15 cm) below the surface to give them access to moisture, even in dry spells. Also, the deeper the root ball, the easier it will be to weed without harming the roots. Fill in the hole with water and soil to about 2 in (5 cm) above the root ball. Wait a couple of weeks and then fill in the rest of the hole with well-rotted compost. Mulch the entire row with a 6-in (15-cm) layer of shredded leaves to stabilize the moisture levels in the soil.

The next spring, thin but recognizable asparagus spears will grow. Do not eat the first year's growth, as the plant needs the energy produced by the ferns to establish a strong root system. Keep the ferns mulched, and apply liquid fish fertilizer every three months during the growing season. Your first harvest will come in the second spring.

Over time, the root systems beneath the soil will multiply, requiring you to dig the crowns up, separate them, and replant in an expanded bed. (They also make great gifts for other gardeners.)

Once your original asparagus bed is four to five years old, wait for late fall when the plant is dormant and dig up the first plant in your row, taking care not to damage the roots. Just do one per year. Gently shake the dirt off to separate the crowns. To replant, for each crown dig a hole 1 foot deep by 1 foot wide (30.5 x 30.5 cm). Blend well-rotted compost and 1 cup (250 mL) Basic Fertilizer Mix (p. 14) in the bottom of the hole and create a conical peak. Spread the roots so they are draped around the peak, and mud the crown in with water, soil, and more compost. Next year, do this for the next plant in the row.

A TIME TO KILL

Weeds are nutrient thieves, evolved to exploit the excellent growing conditions you have created in your garden. They will crowd out your vegetables, steal their food, and spread seeds at their earliest convenience, leaving you to deal with their offspring either immediately or the following year. Deal with weeds before they get a chance to set seed, and you will save yourself a world of pain.

When the soil is warm enough in spring, you can safely till or spade under your green manure and whatever weeds have crept into your garden. Trying to pull weeds from cold, unworked soil is a fool's game. If you aren't going to till your garden, turn weeds upside down by taking a large shovelful of earth around the plant and turning it over so that the roots are facing up and the green top is buried as deeply as possible. Once the freshly turned soil is warmed by the sun, any weeds that survived being turned under will break the surface. This time, however, you are waiting for them, and because the soil is warm and loose, they will come out roots and all.

Summer weeding presents a slightly different challenge, but the same principles apply. Weeds like to sprout from compacted soil in pathways and around delicate vegetables. Working the soil to make raised beds is likely to move a few dormant weed seeds from deep in the soil to nearer the surface, where they will spring to life at the first sign of heat and light. These new sprouts can be dispatched with a sharp hoe.

A few weeds require special treatment: Creeping buttercup, chickweed, and invasive

 Weeds pulled from the garden should be dried in the sun until crisp and brown before composting. Weeds that have gone to seed should be removed with the trash.

morning glory, also known as bindweed. Creeping buttercup is my archenemy. It is wily, invasive, and very tough to eradicate. *Ranunculus repens* is a perennial that will outlive you, unless you kill it first. Creeping buttercup can pop up wherever land is cleared, and it particularly enjoys soils that stay wet most of the year. In dry conditions, it will set seed from bright yellow flowers. If the earth is waterlogged, it sends out runners along the surface of the soil like a strawberry. When the soil is warm and loose, it spreads with startling speed, especially after the soil is worked up. With long, fibrous roots, creeping buttercup can easily survive being chopped up. If you only cut it in half, you'll have twice as many within weeks.

When the weather prediction calls for sun, get up early and water thoroughly. Wait until midday, when the sun has warmed the soil. Use a spade or trowel to loosen the soil about 1 ft (30.5 cm) deep with about 8 in (20 cm) of clearance around each plant. Gently shake the plant to get all the roots up.

Use the same method to remove chickweed, another ground-creeping denizen of disturbed soil. Taking chickweed out early will save you a lot of trouble later in the season. Each plant can set 15,000 seeds, and these seeds can survive in the soil for sixty years.

If you have morning glory anywhere in your yard—I feel your pain. If it is mixed with sod,

you have a big problem. You may need to dig out the morning glory and the sod together and remove them from the property. If it's in your garden, it's almost as bad. Morning glory has roots that can run for 20 ft (6 m) or more and even a ½ inch (1 cm) of root left in the soil will produce a new plant within weeks.

I have covered morning glory with black plastic for two years without eradicating it. But in doing so, all the sod rotted away, and that helped in my mission. Dig widely around the plant, and follow every long, slender, white root as far as you can. If you have a sieve, sift the soil as you go. Bag up the vines and roots, and send them away with the trash. Do not risk your compost by adding morning glory. You may have to revisit the site of a morning glory infestation every few weeks throughout the growing season to completely eradicate it. The key is to sift out every bit of root.

ELIMINATE SOD & EXPAND YOUR GARDEN

In the heat of summer, you can use the sun's energy to kill grassy turf before establishing a new garden or expanding an existing garden. Removing and disposing of live sod is back-breaking work and a waste of useful organic matter. The method I recommend takes a few weeks, but much of that time you can spend in a lawn chair.

Mark the corners of your new garden space with stakes and lengths of string to create a perimeter, then use a weedwacker to scalp the grass right down to the soil. Cover the area with two layers of thick black plastic and secure it with stones and scrap wood so it doesn't blow away. After two weeks of sunny weather, remove the plastic. You should have a patch of mostly

Weeding hoes of Japanese and Dutch design have triangular heads that permit you to work safely in tight spaces. Use a file or grinding burr to put a keen edge on the blade. Draw the hoe along the surface of the soil to slice up newly sprouted weeds.

A winter cover crop of oats, crimson clover, fall rye, or field legumes—or a mix of all of them—will help suppress weeds and provide a lush carpet of green manure to turn under in spring.

dead grass in the early stages of decay. Dust the decaying sod with Basic Fertilizer Mix (p. 14), about 4 cups (1 L) per 100 sq. ft (9.3 sq. m), a 10 x 10 ft (3 x 3 m) area. Turn the sod upside down with a spade and replace the plastic cover. Let the area bake in the sun for two more weeks. This should kill the rest of the grass. The fertilizer you added will accelerate the decomposition of the sod, creating useful soil-enhancing compost. Remove the plastic again, and till or hoe to break down the organic matter. At this point—if it isn't too late in the season—you can amend the soil with compost and plant fall crops such as kale and beets, or put in a cover crop and wait for next spring.

HOW TO CURE POTATOES FOR STORAGE

Potatoes are a terrific way to store food energy, which goes a long way toward explaining their popularity as a home and commercial crop for the past few centuries.

Dry your potatoes for several days before storing. Properly cured potatoes can last many months with no decline in quality, nutrition, or flavor. Improperly cured potatoes will turn into a mess of mold and rot.

Stop watering your potatoes mid-summer. Watch for the vines to wither, then watch the weather forecast, and select a period of at least three sunny, dry days for your harvest. Dig potatoes gently to avoid nicks and abrasions. Do not wash them or attempt to brush the soil away. If you injure the skin before it toughens, you will lose your crop. Most of the dirt will just fall off naturally.

Find a very shady part of the yard for your curing station. I use a spot that is dry and well-protected under dense cedars. Erect a table—a sheet of plywood and a couple of sawhorses works really well—and spread your potatoes out so they are not touching. Cover the potatoes loosely with a tarp to keep out sunlight. Potatoes that are exposed to sunlight may turn green, rendering them inedible.

After three to seven days of dry weather, you can place your potatoes in burlap sacks or well-ventilated cardboard boxes. Store in a very dark, dry, cool place, but protect them from temperatures below 40°F (5°C). Check your potatoes for signs of rot and remove the dodgy ones immediately. Potatoes that are in contact with rotting ones should be washed and eaten as soon as possible.

HOW TO CURE ONIONS FOR STORAGE

When the tops of your storage onions wither, topple, and yellow, it is time to put up your winter supply. Consult a long-term weather report. You will need about a week of dry weather to cure a typical storage onion.

Use a spade or trowel to carefully loosen the soil under and around the bulb. Be careful not to nick the bulbs as they will decay quickly if damaged. Gently pull the bulbs out of the soil and lay them on top of the ground in the sun. You don't need to worry about cleaning them up at this point. Most of the dirt will fall off on its own, and brushing them will damage the skin, which you need intact. After two or three days of sun, most of the tops should be withered. Cut the tops off with sharp clippers.

Set aside the onions with thick, juicy tops, as they are unlikely to cure except in very hot, dry conditions. Just take them inside the house and use them. Move the rest of the onions to a tarp in a sunny part of the yard. The best location is a bit of lawn that is burned dry by the sun. Concrete pads are dry but rough and may damage the onions through the tarp.

Position the onions on half of the tarp so they are not touching. Leave the onions uncovered through the day, then in the evening, before the dew comes, fold the tarp over the onions to keep them dry. Pull back the tarp every morning to expose the onions to the sun. Continue this for about a week, if possible, until the surface skin is brown, dry, and shiny. Remove any onions that show signs of rot or mildew. If the weather turns wet, get the onions inside to a dry location with good air circulation.

Store your onions in a cool, dry place in cardboard boxes, mesh bags, or brown paper bags, stacked no more than three deep.

HOW TO HARVEST GARLIC

Plan to harvest garlic bulbs during a stretch of warm, dry weather. Stop watering them in mid-July to encourage the top to wither and die back. Once the tops are yellow and dry, the soil should be loose and dry. Remove the bulbs by digging underneath them and pulling the entire plant from the ground by the top. Brush them off gently and let them dry in the sun for three days. Carefully trim off the tops and roots, then move to a dry shed for three weeks. Peel off a single layer of papery outer skin, and you will be left with a nice clean bulb. Store garlic bulbs in a cool, dry place.

Basil Pesto

Dark green herbs such as basil and parsley are loaded with potent antioxidants. But who cares? I make pesto more than any other dish in this book simply because everyone loves it. During the summer, when herbs are plentiful, we make pesto and freeze it in 1-cup (250-mL) portions to eat all winter. Toss with hot boiled new potatoes or pasta and top with a sprinkle of cheese.

MAKES 1½ CUPS (375 ML)

½ cup (125 mL) pine nuts

1 firmly packed cup (250 mL) basil

1 firmly packed cup (250 mL) flat-leaf parsley

1 lemon, juiced and zested

½ cup (125 mL) grated Parmesan cheese

2 garlic cloves

½ tsp chili flakes

1 tsp kosher salt

½ tsp pepper

½ cup (125 mL) extra virgin olive oil

Delicious variations: Use walnuts or hazelnuts in place of pine nuts. Use soft herbs such as oregano and marjoram to vary the flavor.

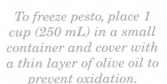

To freeze pesto, place 1 cup (250 mL) in a small container and cover with a thin layer of olive oil to prevent oxidation.

In a dry sauté pan on medium heat, lightly toast pine nuts for 1–2 minutes. In a food processor, place pine nuts, basil, parsley, lemon juice and zest, cheese, garlic, chili, salt, and pepper and pulse to break up pine nuts and garlic. Blend mixture while slowly adding olive oil. Scrape down sides, if necessary. When mixture forms a loose paste, it's done.

Garlic Scape Pesto

Garlic planted in the fall is usually ready for harvest by early August, but to ensure that the plant's energy goes into growing big cloves, you should cut off the scape and seed pod early in July. (The scape is the loopy neck piece with a bulb on the end.) Throw away the bulb and make pesto with the scapes or use them as you would green onions. Toss this pesto with hot pasta or spread on slices of toasted baguette.

MAKES ABOUT I CUP (250 ML)

1 cup (250 mL) chopped scapes

½ cup (125 mL) extra virgin olive oil

2 tbsp lemon juice

½ cup (125 mL) grated Parmesan cheese

¼ tsp ground black pepper

zest of 1 lemon

kosher salt, to taste

Cut garlic scapes into ½-in (1-cm) lengths and add to a vegetable stir-fry.

In a food processor, pulse scapes, oil, and lemon juice until almost smooth. Add cheese, pepper, and lemon zest, and pulse to combine. Taste and season with salt, if desired.

Mashed Pea Bruschetta

This is my reward for planting seeds while my breath is still visible in the air. Get out your very best olive oil for this dish. One bruschetta is a stylish amuse bouche; two pieces make a light appetizer.

MAKES 6 PIECES

1 cup (250 mL) fresh peas

¼ tsp coarse sea salt

¼ cup finely grated Parmesan cheese

¼ cup (60 mL) extra virgin olive oil

1 tbsp lemon juice

6 thin slices baguette

1 garlic clove

ground black pepper, to taste

If you don't have a mortar and pestle, gently pulse the ingredients in a food processor, but avoid over-mixing. We aren't making a purée.

In a large mortar and pestle, mash peas, salt, and cheese. Add just enough olive oil to create a chunky purée with a rich texture. Stir in lemon juice. Toast baguette slices until golden brown and crisp.

Run garlic clove in one light stroke down middle of each slice. (The toast acts like sandpaper.) Spread pea mixture over slices and garnish with a light grind of black pepper and a drizzle of olive oil.

Basil Garlic Dip

This dip is as simple to make as it is delicious to eat. Great with potato chips or vegetable crudités, it also makes an astoundingly good spread for sandwiches. Make it a day ahead and the flavors amplify.

MAKES 1¼ CUPS (310 ML)

1 cup (250 mL) olive oil mayonnaise

1 packed cup (250 mL) basil leaves

¼ cup (60 mL) chopped flat-leaf parsley

1 tbsp lemon juice

1 garlic clove

In a food processor, pulse all ingredients until smooth.

Versatile Cauliflower Soup

Home-grown orange or "cheddar" cauliflower florets are a classic bait and switch. They look like they should taste like cheese curds, but they taste exclusively and intensely of cauliflower in a way that the grocery store version does not. Purple cauliflower makes soup the color of grape soda, which is disconcerting. Avoid it except as a practical joke. This is a very flexible recipe that can take you from vegan to practically meat-atarian.

MAKES 4 SERVINGS

1 tsp extra virgin olive oil

3 garlic cloves, minced

2 shallots, chopped

1 celery stalk, chopped

1 orange cauliflower, chopped

sea or kosher salt, to taste

Add the rind from slab bacon or Parmesan cheese to your soup while it is simmering, then fish it out before you purée. Yum!

Save the rinds from Parmesan cheese in the freezer and toss them in to simmer with soups. If you buy blocks of bacon, save those rinds to sauté with onions when making soups and stews. You don't eat the rinds, but the flavor they add is magic.

In a large pot on medium heat, warm oil. Sauté garlic, shallots, and celery until soft, about 3 minutes. Add cauliflower and 3 cups (750 mL) water or light stock. Bring to a boil, reduce heat to medium-low, and simmer for 30 minutes. Purée with an immersion blender or in a food processor, in small batches. Season to taste with salt.

OPTIONAL DAIRY EMBELLISHMENT:

½ cup (125 mL) cream
1 cup (250 mL) grated cheddar cheese

Prepare soup as above. Whisk in cream and add cheese a little at a time on medium heat until fully incorporated. Top with a little shredded cheddar before serving.

OPTIONAL HIGH-PROTEIN EMBELLISHMENT:

We have made a pretty nice soup at this point, but this is not a meal that will fuel the sort of hard labor that we writers perform on a daily basis. For that, we will need a little more protein. I mean, what if I have to split an infinitive?

1 boneless, skinless chicken breast

½ tsp Randy's All-Purpose Seasoning (p.119)

½ tbsp extra virgin olive oil

4 slices bacon, chopped and fried crispy, drained on paper towel

¼ cup 60 mL) cheddar cheese

¼ cup (60 mL) parsley

Sprinkle chicken breast with seasoning. In a frying pan on medium, heat olive oil. Sauté chicken until cooked through, about 8–10 minutes. Let cool and shred meat. Sprinkle soup with shredded chicken and bacon. Garnish with cheese and chopped parsley.

Fresh Sofrito

This mild but luxurious warm salsa goes with fried potatoes, eggs, and grilled meat. When you hear people talk about food that tastes like itself, this is what they are talking about.

MAKES 2 CUPS (500 ML)

¼ cup (60 mL) extra virgin olive oil

1 cup (250 mL) diced onions

2 garlic cloves, minced

1 jalapeño pepper, seeded and minced

1 red bell pepper, diced

1½ cups (375 mL) diced tomatoes

½ tbsp fresh oregano

1 tsp kosher salt

In a large sauté pan on medium, heat olive oil. Sauté onions until lightly browned. Add garlic, jalapeño, bell pepper, tomatoes, oregano, and salt and simmer until soft, about 5–10 minutes.

Tzatziki Cucumber Salad

Tzatziki is a traditional Greek salad that in North America appears to have has morphed into a sauce of yogurt and garlic not at all like the dish I remember from the Greek islands. My tzatziki is a substantial cucumber salad you can heap on grilled meats and Super Simple Pita Bread (p. 62). Use a tender-skinned cucumber and leave the skin on.

MAKES 2 CUPS (500 ML)

1 large cucumber

1 garlic clove, minced

¼ cup (60 ml) chopped fresh dill fronds

½ tsp coarse sea salt

¼ tsp ground black pepper

⅛ tsp cayenne pepper

¾ cup (120 ml) Greek yogurt

Split cucumber lengthwise and remove seeds with a spoon. Grate cucumber and place in a colander in the sink, then squeeze out excess moisture with your hands. Set aside cucumber to drain.

In a bowl, combine garlic, dill, salt, pepper, cayenne, and yogurt. Stir in cucumber and let mixture sit 15 minutes. Taste and season with more salt, if desired.

Pharoah Salad

Khoresan wheat, known by its brand name Kamut, is an ancient grain that was widely grown in Egypt, Iran, and Afghanistan. It made a big comeback when American farmers started to grow it again in the 1970s for the burgeoning health food market. The grain is rich in fiber and protein, not to mention just about every vitamin and mineral you can name. This salad works well with whatever fresh herbs you have on hand, including cilantro, parsley, mint, dill, oregano, basil, and fennel fronds.

Note: You will need to soak the grains overnight before making this recipe.

MAKES 4 SERVINGS

1 cup (250 mL) Kamut

3 green onions

3 celery stalks

1 medium carrot

1 tbsp lime juice

1 tbsp seasoned rice wine vinegar

2 tbsp extra virgin olive oil

¼ tsp sesame oil

1 tsp coarse sea salt

¼ tsp ground black pepper

2 tbsp chopped cilantro

2 tbsp chopped flat-leaf parsley

1 tbsp chopped fresh mint (optional)

Soak Kamut in 2 cups (500 mL) water for 8 hours or overnight. Drain Kamut and discard water. In a pot on high heat, bring grains and 2 cups (500 mL) fresh water to a boil. Reduce heat to low, cover pot, and simmer for 45 minutes. Drain and set aside to cool.

Dice green onions and celery about ¼–½ in (6 mm–1 cm), close to size of the wheat grains. Peel and coarsely grate carrot.

In a large bowl, whisk together lime juice, vinegar, olive and sesame oil, salt, and pepper. Add Kamut, vegetables, and herbs, and stir to coat. Let marinate for 2 hours before serving.

Farmhouse-Style Sliced Onion Salad

This is one of those recipes that you find on an old index card written by a beloved ancestor who exists today only in memories and in yellowed old photos. Serve it at your next barbecue party and blow people's minds.

MAKES 10–12 SERVINGS

6 large white or Spanish onions

BRINE:

1½ cups (375 mL) water

1½ cups (375 mL) white vinegar

2¼ cups (560 mL) sugar

6 tbsp (90 mL) kosher salt

DRESSING:

1½ cups (375 mL) mayonnaise

3 tbsp celery seeds

1 tsp kosher salt

½ tsp ground black pepper

Reduce your reliance on plastic wrap with reusable wraps made from natural fiber and bee's wax. Look for Abeego, Bee's Wrap, or Apiwraps in health food stores or online.

Peel and slice onions as thinly as possible. Place in a large glass or ceramic bowl. In a large saucepan on high heat, combine water, vinegar, sugar, and salt. Bring to a boil and pour over onions. Let stand for 3–5 hours, then drain thoroughly.

In a large serving bowl, whisk together mayonnaise, celery seeds, salt, and pepper. Add onions and toss to coat. Refrigerate for 3 hours before serving.

Dill Potato Salad

This is the perfect side dish for picnics, barbecues, and balmy evenings, a creamy, herbaceous version of a classic that employs fresh garden dill and last summer's Classic Dill Pickles.

MAKES 6 SERVINGS

2 lb (1 kg) potatoes

1 tbsp kosher salt

3 tbsp chopped fresh dill fronds

1 cup (250 mL) mayonnaise

2 tbsp white wine vinegar

2 tbsp whole grain mustard

½ tsp ground black pepper

¼ tsp kosher salt

2 hard-boiled eggs

½ cup (125 mL) diced green onions

1 cup (250 mL) diced celery

½ cup (125 mL) diced Classic Dill Pickles (p. 132)

To make perfect hard-boiled eggs, bring eggs to a low boil in water for exactly 1 minute, then cover with a lid, turn off burner, and let stand for 11 minutes. Drain and immerse in cold water.

Peel and cube potatoes about ¾ –1 in (2–2.5 cm). In a saucepan on high heat, bring potatoes, 3 cups (750 mL) water, and 1 tbsp salt to a boil. Reduce heat to medium and simmer until knife-tender, about 5 minutes. Drain and set aside to cool.

In a large mixing bowl, combine dill, mayonnaise, vinegar, mustard, pepper, and salt. Peel and chop eggs. Add eggs, green onions, celery, and pickles to mixture. Add potatoes and use a rubber spatula to gently fold mixture until evenly coated with dressing.

If desired, garnish top of salad with more chopped dill, diced green onions, slices of hard-boiled eggs, and a dusting of paprika. Serve immediately or keep refrigerated until mealtime.

Zero-Fat Salad Dressing

The light, bright flavor of this dressing makes your salad a palate-cleansing counterpoint to a rich entrée. Toss with fresh salad greens.

MAKES ½ CUP (125 ML)

1 tomato, minced

1 green onion, minced

1 tsp lime juice

½ tsp sea salt

1 tbsp chopped cilantro leaves

In a bowl, combine all ingredients. Let mixture sit for 5 minutes.

Choose Sustainable Seafood

As a lover of seafood, I worry about the state of the world's oceans. Many fisheries are overtaxed and some have been fished to extinction, but the tide is starting to turn. Sustainability certifications provide some assurance that the fish you buy in stores and restaurants come from healthy, well-managed fisheries.

SeaChoice (*seachoice.org*) is a consortium of non-profit scientific and environmental groups that monitors fisheries for ecological integrity and offers ratings of Best Choice, Some Concerns, and Avoid. Couldn't be easier.

Seafood Watch (*seafoodwatch.org*), a project of the Monterey Bay Aquarium in California, offers a searchable list of common sea foods, including information about the state of the fishery, a description of how the fish is caught, and a sustainability rating.

Ocean Wise (*oceanwise.ca*) is a conservation program from the Vancouver Aquarium that provides detailed information about West Coast fisheries as well as a useful list of Canadian restaurants that serve sustainable seafood.

Marine Stewardship Council (*msc.org*) is an independent non-profit organization working with fisheries, distributors, and retailers all over the world on certification of sustainable fisheries and product traceability. MSC employs a science-based approach to fishery standards and best practices for industry. Certified products carry a recognizable dark blue label.

Fried Halibut with Tartar Sauce

This is a very simple treatment for halibut that approximates the fish 'n' chips experience without an oil-soaked batter. Panko bread crumbs make the fish super crisp. I developed this recipe for my mother-in-law, who likes her fish firm, thoroughly cooked, and crunchy. Serve with Seasoned Oven Fries (p. 103) and Tartar Sauce.

MAKES 4–6 SERVINGS

canola oil, for frying

2 lb (1 kg) halibut fillet

5 tsp Randy's All-Purpose Seasoning (p. 119)

1 cup (250 mL) all-purpose flour

2 eggs

2½ cups (625 mL) panko bread crumbs

TARTAR SAUCE:

½ cup (125 mL) mayonnaise

3 tbsp Old-Fashioned Relish (p. 133)

½ tsp Louisiana-style hot sauce or Sriracha

½ tsp yellow mustard

The Pacific halibut stock is in good shape—just off a thirty-year high—and there are relatively few concerns about the effects of the long lines used to harvest them. Of all your halibut choices, Pacific is the way to go.

Preheat ½ in (1 cm) canola oil to 340°F (170°C) in a high-sided frying pan. Cut halibut into slices 1-in (2.5-cm) thick. Season on all sides with 2 tsp seasoning. Place flour on a plate. In a wide bowl, whisk eggs.

On a separate plate, season panko with remaining 3 tsp seasoning. With your left hand, dredge a fillet in flour, then roll it in beaten eggs. Lift fillet with left hand and allow excess egg to run off. Use right hand to dredge in panko and place gently into hot oil. (Be careful when working with hot oil, and don't let it splash!) Fry fish for 2 minutes, until golden brown, then turn and fry for another 2 minutes, until firm to the touch.

TARTAR SAUCE:

In a bowl, mix all ingredients until combined. Set aside for 15 minutes.

Makes ⅔ cup (160 mL).

Pasta with Cherry Tomato Tuna Sauce

Pasta with tuna sauce is a popular, home-style Italian dish that has not migrated to the New World. This simple recipe gives you a rich dressing for pasta that is brimming with healthy stuff. It takes no more time to cook than does your pasta. Use good Italian tinned tuna packed in olive oil and make sure to use the olive oil from the tin to enhance the tuna flavor. I use tripolina lunga noodles, which are like long skinny lasagna noodles with ruffled edges. Fresh linguini or fettuccini would also be terrific.

MAKES 2 MEAL-SIZED SERVINGS

2 garlic cloves, minced

1 shallot, minced

1 small red chili pepper, seeded

5.6 oz (160 g) oil-packed tuna (reserve oil)

1 cup (250 mL) halved cherry tomatoes

¼ cup (60mL) fresh peas

½ lb (250 g) pasta

¼ cup (60 mL) grated Pecorino cheese

¼ cup (60 mL) chopped flat-leaf parsley

The Rio Mare brand tuna uses yellowfin, which is considered resilient to fishing pressure. It's certified by SeaChoice as a sustainable Best Choice.

In a large pot on high, bring 1 gal (4 L) water and 1½ tbsp kosher salt to a boil.

Meanwhile, in a large sauté pan (large enough to accommodate cooked pasta) on medium-low heat, sauté garlic, shallot, chilies, and oil from tuna for 3 minutes. Add tuna and tomatoes. Increase heat to medium. Simmer for 5 minutes, until tomatoes soften. Use back of a wooden spoon to lightly mash tomatoes and tuna together. Add peas and turn off burner.

To pot of boiling water, add pasta and cook according to package directions. Drain pasta and reserve ¼ cup (60 mL) cooking liquid. Stir in cooked pasta and cheese with tomato-tuna mixture and toss while adding reserved cooking liquid. Sprinkle with parsley.

Frittata, Three Ways

Frittatas are the only way I know to use leftovers so that you end up with something classy enough to serve to company. There are two components to frittata: the essential elements (eggs, fried potatoes, cheese, and olive oil) and your embellishments. Whatever embellishments you choose to add, chop them so that they are no bigger than a marble and are cooked and heated through before the eggs go in.

ALL VERSIONS MAKE 4 SERVINGS

SAUSAGE & PEPPER FRITTATA:

1 tbsp extra virgin olive oil

1 cup (250 mL) cooked diced potatoes

2 cooked spicy Italian sausages, sliced

1/3 cup (80 mL) julienned red bell peppers

1/3 cup (80 mL) sliced white mushrooms

1/3 cup (80 mL) diced onions

1/3 cup (80 mL) chopped green onions

1 tsp kosher salt, divided

6 large eggs

1/2 cup (250 mL) grated Asiago cheese

Preheat oven to 350°F (180°C).

In a large non-stick, oven-proof frying pan on medium, heat olive oil. Add potatoes and fry until lightly browned. Add sausages and fry for 2 minutes. Add peppers, mushrooms, onions, and green onions, and 1/2 tsp salt. Toss to combine and heat through, about 2–3 minutes. Whisk eggs with remainder of salt and pour over sausage mixture. Gently shake frying pan to work eggs through mixture. Sprinkle cheese evenly over top. Bake for 7–9 minutes, until middle is firm. Slide frittata onto a plate and serve in wedges.

SALMON & DILL FRITTATA:

1 tbsp extra virgin olive oil

1 cup (250 mL) cooked diced potatoes

6–8 oz (175–230 g) cooked salmon

6 large eggs

½ tsp kosher salt

2 tsp Louisiana-style hot sauce

3 tbsp chopped fresh dill fronds

2 green onions, chopped

½ cup (125 mL) grated Gruyère cheese

Preheat oven to 350°F (180°C).

In a large non-stick, oven-proof frying pan on medium, heat olive oil. Add potatoes and salmon and cook about 2–3 minutes.

In a mixing bowl, whisk eggs, salt, hot sauce, and dill, and pour over salmon mixture. Sprinkle on green onions and cheese. Gently shake frying pan to work eggs through mixture. Bake for 7–9 minutes, until middle is firm. Slide frittata onto a plate and serve in wedges.

GREEN EGGS & HAM:

1 tbsp extra virgin olive oil

½ cup (125 mL) chopped prosciutto

¾ cup (185 mL) cooked diced potatoes

¼ cup (60 mL) diced red bell peppers

¼ cup (60 mL) chopped green onions

6 eggs

½ cup (125 mL) Basil Pesto (p. 76)

½ tsp salt

¼ tsp ground black pepper

¼ cup (60 mL) grated Pecorino cheese

A hit at any Seuss-themed event, served hot or cold.

Preheat oven to 350°F (180°C).

In a large non-stick, oven-proof pan on medium, heat olive oil and prosciutto. Fry until crispy, about 4–5 minutes.

Remove prosciutto from pan and set aside. Add potatoes and fry until golden brown, about 5–6 minutes. Add peppers and green onions, and sauté for 2 minutes. Return prosciutto to pan.
In a mixing bowl, whisk eggs, pesto, salt, and pepper and pour over prosciutto mixture. Gently shake frying pan to work eggs through mixture. Sprinkle with cheese. Bake for 7–9 minutes, until middle is firm. Slide frittata onto a plate and serve in wedges.

Beef Enchiladas with Fresh Mexican Tomato Sauce

Most commercially prepared sauces and condiments are loaded with salt, and many also contain high-fructose corn syrup (often under its many obscure names). Fresh Mexican Tomato Sauce is loaded with natural flavor. Top with Pico de Gallo & Guacamole (p. 31).

MAKES 6 SERVINGS

FRESH MEXICAN TOMATO SAUCE:

3 cups (750 mL) diced tomatoes

1 roasted red bell pepper (p. 45), diced

¼ tsp chipotle powder

2 garlic cloves, minced

2 dried pasilla or ancho chilies, seeded

½ tsp dried oregano

1 tsp ground cumin

1 tbsp honey

1 tbsp fresh cilantro leaves

1 tsp kosher salt

BEEF ENCHILADAS:

1 tbsp extra virgin olive oil

1 lb (500 g) lean ground beef

1 cup (250 mL) minced onions

1 tsp kosher salt

2½ cups (625 mL) Fresh Mexican Tomato Sauce

2 cups (500 mL) cooked black beans

12 white corn tortillas

2 cups (500 mL) grated Monterey Jack cheese

FRESH MEXICAN TOMATO SAUCE:

In a large saucepan on medium-high heat, combine all ingredients with 1 cup (250 mL) water. Bring to a low boil, then reduce heat and simmer for 20 minutes. Blend with an immersion blender or, in a food processor, purée in small batches to make a smooth sauce.

BEEF ENCHILADAS:

Preheat oven to 350°F (180°C).

In a large saucepan on medium, heat olive oil. Add beef, onions, and salt, breaking up meat until cooked through, about 10 minutes. Add ¾ cup (185 mL) Tomato Sauce and beans and simmer for 10 minutes. Mash half of the black beans with back of a spoon, until mixture thickens. Spread ¼ cup (60 mL) Tomato Sauce on bottom of a 9 x 12 in (23 x 30.5 cm) baking dish.

Turn burner on stovetop to medium heat. Place 1 tortilla at a time on heated burner, moving it with tongs every 15 seconds as it steams and chars. Toast for 20–30 seconds on each side, place on a plate, and cover with a tea towel. Repeat with remaining tortillas.

To assemble enchiladas: Place 1 tortilla on a plate and smear both sides with ½ tbsp sauce. Place ⅓ cup (80 mL) beef and bean filling on tortilla. Roll tortilla over filling away from you. Place rolled tortilla in casserole dish. Repeat with remainder of tortillas and filling. Pour remainder of sauce over top and sprinkle evenly with cheese. Cover loosely with foil and bake for 30 minutes. Remove foil and broil on high until cheese bubbles. Let stand for 10 minutes before serving.

Malai Kofta in Tomato-Ginger Sauce

These nutty vegetarian meatballs are served across northern India, but they are hard to find in North America. Now that paneer—a home-style Indian cheese—is available in many grocery stores, it is possible to replicate this amazing dish at home. For a vegan meal, replace paneer with extra-firm tofu. Serve with basmati rice.

MAKES 4 SERVINGS

TOMATO-GINGER SAUCE:

2 tbsp canola oil

1 cup (250 mL) diced onions

2 tbsp grated fresh ginger

2 garlic cloves, minced

1½ tbsp minced, seeded jalapeño pepper

1 tsp ground cumin

2 tsp ground coriander

3 cups (750 mL) diced fresh tomatoes

1½ tsp kosher salt

3 tbsp ground pistachios

½ cup (125 mL) sour cream or plain yogurt

KOFTAS:

2 cups (500 mL) diced, cooked potatoes

½ cup (125 mL) ground pistachios

¾ cup (185 mL) finely grated carrots

2 tsp ground coriander

1 tsp ground cumin

5 oz (150 g) paneer, coarsely grated

1½ tbsp minced, seeded jalapeños

3 tbsp fresh cilantro leaves

¼ tsp cayenne pepper

1½ tsp kosher salt

3 cups (750 mL) canola oil, for frying

chopped pistachios, for garnish

TOMATO-GINGER SAUCE:

In a sauté pan on medium, heat canola oil. Sauté onions until golden brown, about 6 minutes. Stir in ginger, garlic, jalapeño, cumin, and coriander, and cook for 1 minute. Add tomatoes, ¼ cup (60 mL) water, and salt, and heat until mixture bubbles vigorously. Reduce heat to medium-low and simmer for 10–15 minutes. Remove from heat, and stir in ground pistachios and sour cream. Mash until smooth or purée with an immersion blender.

KOFTAS:

In a food processor, add potatoes, ground pistachios, carrots, coriander, cumin, paneer, jalapeños, cilantro, cayenne, and salt. Pulse processor to chop ingredients, scraping down sides as needed. Then turn processor to high until mixture forms a firm, tacky ball, about 30–60 seconds.

To make koftas, roll 2 tbsp mixture at a time between your palms to form balls. Place on a cookie sheet, then refrigerate for 1 hour.

In a deep pot on medium, heat canola oil to 350°F (180°C). Deep-fry koftas, 4 pieces at a time, for 3 minutes, until browned. Remove to plate covered with a paper towel to drain.

Divide Tomato-Ginger sauce between 4 bowls and top with 3 koftas. Garnish with chopped pistachios.

I dedicate an electric coffee grinder to crushing whole spices and making pistachio flour. If you don't have a grinder, substitute store-bought almond flour for ground pistachios in this recipe.

Toasting whole cumin and coriander seeds in a dry pan for 1 minute before grinding will greatly enhance their flavor.

Baked Polenta

To save time, make Sweet Corn Polenta and spread on a cookie sheet the day before. Refrigerate overnight, then bake for dinner. Serve with grilled sausage or Chicken alla Cacciatore (p. 186).

MAKES 4 SERVINGS

1 tbsp canola oil

5 cups (1.25 L) Sweet Corn Polenta (p. 100)

1 tomato, thinly sliced

½ cup (125 mL) grated Parmesan cheese

¼ tsp ground black pepper

Preheat oven to 450°F (230°C).

Oil a 9 x 15 in (23 x 28 cm) cookie sheet with canola oil. Cover with parchment paper, trimmed to fit. Prepare Sweet Corn Polenta and pour onto cookie sheet. Smooth with a rubber spatula and set aside to cool for 30 minutes (or refrigerate overnight).

Top polenta with tomato slices, cheese, and pepper. Bake on middle rack of oven until edges are browned, about 30 minutes.

Sweet Corn Polenta

Polenta is essentially ground corn porridge. In Italy, it is flavored with stock and aged cheese such as provolone. Eaten hot, polenta is a creamy side dish that complements saucy, slow-cooked Osso Buco (p. 190). When you spread polenta on a sheet to cool, it sets up firm enough to fry or bake (p. 99).

MAKES 5 CUPS (1.25 L)

2 large ears corn, to yield 1–1½ cups (250–375 mL) corn kernels

4 cups (1 L) low-sodium chicken stock or water

½ tsp kosher salt

1 cup (250 mL) quick-cooking polenta

1 roasted red bell pepper (p. 45), diced

1½ tbsp minced, seeded jalapeño peppers

¼ cup (60 mL) butter

½ cup (125 mL) grated Parmesan cheese

Roast the red pepper on your barbecue at the same time as the corn, on the hottest part of the grill.

Preheat barbecue to high. Peel and roast corn whole on a hot grill, turning every 2 minutes until kernels begin to brown, about 10 minutes. Hold corn cob by the stalk, and use a sharp knife to cut kernels from cob. Set corn aside.

In a large saucepan on medium-high heat, bring stock or water to a low boil and add salt. (If using water, add additional ½ tsp salt.) Add polenta, stirring continuously until mixture thickens, about 3 minutes. Reduce heat to low and stir in corn, bell pepper, jalapeños, butter, and cheese. Taste and season with salt and pepper, if desired. Thin to a creamy texture with water, stock, or cream, if necessary. Serve immediately.

Sofrito Poached Eggs

This is my garden-fresh take on the Mexican classic huevos rancheros. Serve it with refried beans and tortilla chips, with Tapas-Style Fried Potatoes (p. 102), or just a side of crispy toast.

MAKES 2–4 SERVINGS

2 cups (500 mL) Fresh Sofrito (p. 82)   4 large eggs

In a large sauté pan with a tight-fitting lid on medium-low, simmer Fresh Sofrito. Make 4 spaces in sauce, about 4 in (10 cm) across. Break an egg into each one. Cover and steam for about 4 minutes, or until whites are cooked.

Tapas-Style Fried Potatoes

Fried potatoes come to life when they meet their good friend chorizo. This is the sort of snack you see at bodegas throughout Spain, though the ingredients vary by region. Smoked paprika is a Spanish specialty with dimensions of flavor you can only imagine until you try it for yourself. It would also be culturally appropriate to substitute thinly sliced Serrano-style ham for the chorizo. Serve with Fresh Sofrito (p. 82).

MAKES 4 SERVINGS

1½ lb (750 g) Yukon Gold potatoes, diced

1 3-oz (90-g) cured chorizo sausage

   (1 sausage about 5 in/13 cm long)

2 tbsp extra virgin olive oil

½ tsp smoked paprika

½ tsp sea salt

¼ cup (60 mL) chopped green onions

1 tbsp cilantro leaves

In a large pot on high heat, bring potatoes with enough cold water to cover and 1 tsp kosher salt to a boil, then simmer for 3 minutes. Drain potatoes and set aside.

Slice chorizo ⅛-in (3-mm) thick. In a large frying pan on medium, heat olive oil. Add chorizo slices and fry until crisp. Remove chorizo from pan and set aside. Increase heat to medium-high and fry cooked potatoes, turning every 2–3 minutes until crisp, about 10 minutes. Add paprika and salt, and toss to coat.

Transfer potatoes to a serving plate and sprinkle with chorizo slices, green onions, and cilantro.

Seasoned Oven Fries

These spicy wedges are the perfect side on steak night. They taste great beside a hamburger, too. Serve with Fresh Tomato Catsup (p. 120).

MAKES 4–6 SERVINGS

2 lb (1 kg) Yukon Gold potatoes

2 tsp Randy's All-Purpose Seasoning (p. 119)

2 tbsp extra virgin olive oil

Preheat oven to 425°F (220°C).

Wash potatoes in cold water and cut into wedges ½ in (1 cm) thick. Dry wedges on a tea towel and place in a bowl with seasoning and olive oil. Toss to coat.

Arrange wedges on a baking sheet, with space between each. Place baking sheet on middle rack of oven and bake for 20 minutes. Turn wedges over and bake for another 15 minutes, until they are golden brown.

Salad Rolls
with Spicy Peanut Sauce

I love the crunch and freshness of Southeast Asian cooking, and salad rolls bring it all together as a hand-held vegetable-delivery system. My salad rolls make a light meal or a party platter with spicy dipping sauce.

SPICY PEANUT SAUCE:

½ cup (125 mL) smooth peanut butter

⅓ cup (80 mL) hot water

1 tsp cayenne pepper

2 tbsp light soy sauce

2 tbsp seasoned rice vinegar

¼ cup (60 mL) chopped green onions or chives

SALAD ROLLS:

3.5 oz (100 g) rice vermicelli

3 tbsp seasoned rice vinegar, divided

1 cup (250 mL) grated carrots

¼ cup (60 mL) Spicy Peanut Sauce

1 cup (250 mL) shredded cooked chicken

10 8-in (20-cm) round rice paper wrappers

½ cup (125 mL) chopped green onions

1 cup (250 mL) bean sprouts

½ cup (125 mL) cilantro leaves

1½ cups (375 mL) sliced Napa cabbage

SPICY PEANUT SAUCE:

In a mixing bowl, combine peanut butter with hot water. Whisk gently until smooth. Stir in cayenne, soy sauce, and vinegar, then stir in green onions.

SALAD ROLLS:

In a large bowl, place vermicelli. Add 1 qt/L boiling water and let the noodles soften for 3–5 minutes, until tender but firm. Drain and set aside to cool. Add 2 tbsp vinegar to vermicelli and toss to combine.

Line up filling ingredients in bowls in the order given. Add 1 tbsp vinegar to carrots. Add Peanut Sauce to chicken and stir to coat.

Place a lint-free cotton tea towel on work surface. Fill a pie plate with hot water and immerse 1 wrapper at a time in water for 20–30 seconds. Lay wrapper flat on tea towel and add 1 tbsp carrots in a line 5 in (12 cm) long. Add ½ tbsp green onions, 1 tbsp sprouts, 4–5 cilantro leaves, 1½ tbsp chicken, and 1½ tbsp cabbage. Fold wrapper over filling, away from you. Fold sides in to close ends, then gently press down on filling and roll wrapper away from you to form a tube.

Chiang Mai Noodles

Chiang Mai was a sleepy town in northern Thailand when I went there in the '80s. Backpackers and monkeys scurried everywhere, stealing what they could. What I really liked about Chiang Mai was the fact that you were never more than a few steps from noodles. A "restaurant" just around the corner from our guest house had a canvas roof held up by a few poles and contained simply a gas ring and a wok. I remember their plates of noodles fondly, though I had to beg them to stop sprinkling white sugar over my noodles, which perplexed them. This recipe does not call for sugar.

MAKES 2–4 SERVINGS

5.6 oz (160 g) dried medium rice sticks

6 oz (175 g) firm tofu

4 tbsp canola oil, divided

5 garlic cloves, minced

1 dried red chili pepper, crumbled

¼ tsp kosher salt

1 cup (250 mL) sliced mushrooms

1 cup (250 mL) Napa cabbage, thinly sliced

¼ cup (60 mL) julienned red bell peppers

¼ cup (60 mL) julienned green bell peppers

1 cup (250 mL) chopped chard leaves or spinach

2 tsp fish sauce

1 tbsp chili-garlic sauce

½ lime

2 green onions, chopped

¼ cup (60 mL) chopped dry-roasted peanuts

In a bowl filled with boiling water, soften rice noodles according to package directions. Drain noodles and set aside.

Cut tofu into ½-in (1-cm) cubes. In a wok on high, heat 2 tbsp canola oil. Fry tofu cubes until golden brown, 3–4 minutes. Reduce heat to medium. Stir in garlic, chili, and salt, and toss ingredients while cooking for 1 minute. Remove tofu mixture from wok and set aside. Return wok to medium-high, and heat 2 tbsp oil. Add mushrooms and let them sit undisturbed for about 1 minute, until lightly browned. Stir in cabbage, peppers, and chard, and toss while cooking for 2 minutes. Add fish sauce, chili-garlic sauce, and softened noodles, turning to coat. Squeeze lime over noodles and top with green onions, fried tofu, and peanuts.

Spinach & Feta Penne

I like the Greek flavors in this quick, fresh lunch. The sauce takes no longer to cook than the pasta, so get your water boiling first, and you'll being eating in 10 minutes flat.

MAKES 4 SERVINGS

2 tbsp kosher salt

¼ cup (60 mL) extra virgin olive oil

4 garlic cloves, sliced

2 cups (500 mL) diced fresh tomatoes

6 cups (1.5 L) fresh spinach leaves

1 lb (500 g) dried penne

1 cup (250 mL) crumbled feta cheese

½ cup (125 mL) pitted kalamata olives

½ cup (125 mL) pine nuts

To remove the pit from a Kalamata olive, press down on the olive with the flat side of your chef knife until the flesh gives way. Fold back the sides of the olive with your fingers and remove the pit.

In a large pot on high heat, add kosher salt to 6 qt/L water and bring to a boil. (It's important to have the right amount of salt in the water as it seasons the pasta and later the sauce.)

Add penne and cook until tender but firm, about 8–10 minutes.

Meanwhile, in a large heavy-bottomed pan on medium, heat olive oil. Sauté garlic and tomatoes until soft, about 5 minutes. Stir in spinach and turn until wilted, about 3 minutes.

Drain pasta, reserving 1 cup (250 mL) cooking liquid. Add cooked penne, feta cheese, olives, pine nuts, and reserved cooking liquid to spinach sauce. Toss to form a light sauce.

Linguini with Creamy Pesto Sauce

I borrowed the idea for this luxurious pesto from an old trattoria in Vancouver's Little Italy. As is the case for most Italian dishes, its greatness lies in its simplicity. Let the fresh basil sing.

MAKES 4 SERVINGS

2 tbsp kosher salt

¾ cup (185 mL) cream

½ cup (125 mL) grated Parmesan cheese

½ tsp kosher salt

1 cup (250 mL) Basil Pesto (p. 76)

1 lb (500 g) dried linguini

In a large sauté pan on medium-low heat, warm cream, ¼ cup (60 mL) cheese, and ½ tsp salt to a low simmer. Add Basil Pesto and stir to heat through. Taste and season with more salt, if desired.

In a large pot on high heat, add 2 tbsp kosher salt to 6 qt/L water and bring to a boil.

Add linguini and cook until tender but firm, about 8–10 minutes. Drain and toss with sauce. Sprinkle each serving with about 1 tbsp Parmesan cheese.

Fancy Broccoli

I have been doing this dish for so long that I can't remember where I got the idea in the first place. It's a great way to treat broccoli, asparagus, gai lan, or broccolini, and it looks right at home with a fancy meal or on a plain old Tuesday night. Use whatever small ripe tomatoes you have on hand.

MAKES 4 SERVINGS

1 tbsp extra virgin olive oil

1 garlic clove, minced

4 cups (1 L) broccoli florets

⅓ cup (80 mL) white wine

1 cup (250 mL) chopped Roma tomatoes

½ tsp kosher salt

1 tbsp butter

In a large sauté pan on medium, heat olive oil. Sauté garlic until fragrant, no more than 30 seconds. Increase heat to medium-high and add broccoli and wine. Cover with a tight-fitting lid and cook for 3 minutes. Remove broccoli from pan and set aside.

Add tomatoes and salt and sauté until tomatoes soften, then mash tomatoes with the back of a spoon to form a sauce. Remove from heat and stir in butter until melted. Add broccoli and toss to coat.

Tamil Turnip Greens

This spicy Tamil-style dish answers the question:
What am I going to do with the top half of my turnips?

MAKES 4–6 SERVINGS

2 tbsp butter

1 leek, halved and thinly sliced

2 garlic cloves, thinly sliced

1 green serrano or jalapeño pepper, seeded and minced

½ tsp ground turmeric

1 tsp mustard seeds

1 tsp ground cumin

1 lb (500 g) turnip greens, roughly chopped

½ cup (125 mL) low-sodium chicken or vegetable stock

1 tsp kosher salt, divided

In a large saucepan on medium, heat butter until solids separate from fat. Add leeks and garlic and sauté until soft, 3–5 minutes. Add serrano, turmeric, mustard seeds, and cumin, and sauté for 1 minute.

Add turnip greens, stock, and ½ tsp salt. Turn greens until they wilt, then simmer for 15 minutes. Taste and season with remainder of salt, if desired.

Green Beans
with Shallots & Almonds

Transform fresh green beans into a memorable side that is naturally sweet, salty, and aromatic.

MAKES 6 SERVINGS

1 lb (500 g) green beans, trimmed

2 tbsp extra virgin olive oil

⅓ cup (80 mL) thinly sliced shallots

⅓ cup (80 mL) slivered almonds

½ tsp kosher salt

⅛ tsp ground black pepper

1 tbsp lemon zest

2 tbsp chopped fresh parsley

In a large pot of boiling water on high heat, blanch beans for 3 minutes. Drain and immerse in a bath of cold water and ice cubes. Drain beans and set aside.

In a large sauté pan on medium, heat olive oil. Sauté shallots until golden, then add almonds and cook while stirring for 1 minute. Add green beans, salt, pepper, and lemon zest, and cook until green beans are heated through, about 1–2 minutes. Remove from heat. Sprinkle with parsley.

Jamaican Rice & Peas

This is a great side for spicy grilled chicken or pork, or as a vegetarian lunch all on its own.

MAKES 4 SERVINGS

½ cup (125 mL) dried black-eyed peas

2 tbsp extra virgin olive oil

4 garlic cloves, minced

1 tsp fresh thyme

1 jalapeño pepper, seeded and minced

¼ cup (60 mL) diced red bell peppers

½ tsp ground black pepper

½ tsp ground allspice

½ cup (125 mL) chopped green onions, divided

1 cup (250 mL) basmati rice

1½ cups (375 mL) low-sodium chicken stock

1 tsp kosher salt

In a saucepan on high heat, bring black-eyed peas to a boil in 2 cups (500 mL) unsalted fresh water. Reduce heat to medium-low and simmer for about 40 minutes, until tender but firm. Drain and set aside.

In a large saucepan on medium heat, combine olive oil, garlic, thyme, jalapeño, bell peppers, black pepper, allspice, and ¼ cup (60 mL) chopped green onions. Sauté for 3–4 minutes. Add rice and stir to coat with oil. Add stock and salt and increase heat to high. Taste liquid and adjust seasoning with more salt, if desired. When liquid comes to a boil, cover pot with lid, reduce heat to low, and cook for 10 minutes. Turn off heat and leave pot on burner for another 10 minutes. Remove lid and fluff up rice with a fork. Top with remaining green onions.

Strawberry-Rhubarb Pie

Pie is the ideal way to celebrate the first fruit of the season. Let's face it—pie is good anytime. Rhubarb is one of the first plants you can harvest in spring, but the good news is that it remains productive right through the growing season.

MAKES 8 SERVINGS

PASTRY:

3 cups (750 mL) all-purpose flour

½ tsp brown sugar

1 tsp kosher salt

1 cup (250 mL) frozen butter

⅔ cup (160 mL) cold water, plus extra if needed

STRAWBERRY-RHUBARB FILLING:

1½ cups (375 mL) sugar

⅓ cup (80 mL) cornstarch

1 tsp ground cinnamon

3 cups (750 mL) diced rhubarb

2½ cups (625 mL) diced strawberries

1 tbsp grated fresh ginger

GLAZE:

1 large egg, beaten

1 tbsp white sugar

If you use frozen rhubarb to make a pie or crisp, first make sure it is completely thawed, then squeeze out any excess moisture or your dessert will be runny.

In a large mixing bowl, combine flour, brown sugar, and salt. Grate butter over flour and toss to combine. Add ¼ cup (60 mL) water and stir with a fork. Add remainder of water 1 tbsp at a time as needed until a dough forms. Divide dough in half and wrap in cling film. Refrigerate for at least 1 hour.

Preheat oven to 425°F (220°C).

Sprinkle flour on working surface and roll out 1 piece of dough large enough to cover pie plate with an extra ¼-in (6-mm) border. Place rolled dough in pie plate and adjust to fit. Flour working surface and roll second piece of dough to same size as first. Cut into 10¾-in (2-cm) wide strips.

In a bowl, combine sugar, cornstarch, and cinnamon. In a large mixing bowl, combine rhubarb, strawberries, and ginger. Add dry ingredients and toss to coat. Immediately fill pie plate with fruit mixture. Build a lattice top (see sidebar) and brush with egg wash, then sprinkle with 1 tbsp sugar for glaze. Bake for 45 minutes, until filling bubbles and the crust is golden brown. Let pie cool for 1 hour before slicing.

To make a lattice top, lay five strips of dough vertically across top of filling. Fold back 1st, 3rd, and 5th strips halfway, and lay 1 strip of dough horizontally across middle of pie. That's the equator. Unfold the 3 strips. Now fold back 2nd and 4th vertical strips and lay down a 2nd horizontal strip above first. Unfold the 2 strips.

Fold back 1st, 3rd, and 5th strips and lay down another strip of dough, then unfold the strips. Repeat procedure south of equator. Trim overhang with a sharp knife and, using your thumbs and forefingers, crimp ends of strips to create a fluted pattern all the way around.

Spicy Zucchini Scones

These fluffy scones are delicious with soups and stews and they freeze exceptionally well.

MAKES 8–10 SCONES

3 cups (750 mL) all-purpose flour

4 tsp baking powder

1 tsp kosher salt

½ tsp baking soda

½ tsp cayenne pepper

½ tsp garlic powder

1 cup (250 mL) grated zucchini

¾ cup (185 mL) grated cheddar cheese

¼ cup (60 mL) chopped chives

¼ cup (60 mL) chopped fresh parsley

2 tbsp chopped fresh dill fronds

2 eggs

1 cup (250 mL) buttermilk

4 tbsp melted butter

Preheat oven to 350°F (180°C).

In a large mixing bowl, whisk together flour, baking powder, salt, baking soda, cayenne, and garlic powder. Add zucchini, cheese, chives, parsley, and dill, and toss to combine.

In a separate bowl, whisk together eggs, buttermilk, and melted butter, then add to flour mixture. Mix lightly with a fork just until a wet dough forms (the dough need not be smooth).

Line a cookie sheet with parchment paper and spoon ½ cup (125 mL) dough for each scone, leaving space between them. Bake until lightly browned and a toothpick inserted in thickest part of scone comes out clean, about 40 minutes.

Quick Fridge Relish

Late in the summer, the bell peppers and onions are ripening in large numbers, but tomatoes take a little longer. This relish will make use of a few green tomatoes and requires no canning equipment. It keeps for a couple of weeks in the fridge, but it's so good, it'll be gone before then.

MAKES 2½ CUPS (625 ML)

1 tbsp extra virgin olive oil

1 cup (250 mL) minced onions

½ cup minced yellow bell peppers

1 jalapeño pepper, seeded and minced

1 garlic clove, minced

½ tsp celery seeds

¼ tsp mustard seeds

⅛ tsp ground cloves

2 tbsp white sugar

2 tbsp sherry vinegar

1 tbsp lemon juice

2 cups (500 mL) minced green tomatoes

1 tbsp chopped fresh dill fronds

2 tsp kosher salt

¼ tsp ground black pepper

In a saucepan on medium, heat olive oil. Add onions and sauté until soft. Stir in yellow peppers, jalapeño, garlic, celery and mustard seeds, and cloves. Simmer for 2 minutes.

Stir in sugar, vinegar, and lemon juice and heat through. Stir in tomatoes, dill, salt, and pepper and simmer for 10 minutes. Add water 1 tbsp at a time if the mixture is too thick.

Randy's All-Purpose Seasoning

Use this simple spice mix for chicken, potatoes, seafood, or pork.
It brings a lot to the table.

MAKES ¾ CUP (185 ML)

2 tbsp Hungarian paprika

1 tbsp hot smoked paprika

3 tbsp kosher salt

1 tsp ground black pepper

2 tbsp onion powder

1 tsp garlic powder

2 tsp cumin

2 tsp dried oregano

1 tbsp dried thyme leaves

Combine all ingredients in a
jar with a lid. Seal and shake.
Use generously.

Fresh Tomato Catsup

How local is your burger? Home-grown lettuce and tomatoes are a good start. Home preserves like relish and pickles—even better. You can certainly buy local pasture-raised beef. This tangy, homemade catsup is the next logical step.

MAKES 1½ CUPS (375 ML)

2 lb (1 kg) plum tomatoes, diced

1 dried pasilla pepper, seeded

1 dried chipotle pepper, seeded

½ cup (125 mL) apple cider vinegar

1 tsp kosher salt

2 tsp mustard powder

½ tsp ground allspice

¼ tsp ground cloves

½ cup (125 mL) liquid honey

½ cup (125 mL) tomato paste

One way to control sodium or sugar in your diet is by taking control of what's in your catsup. This recipe has very little salt compared with commercial products and no high-fructose corn syrup. You can easily adjust it to taste. San Marzano or Roma tomatoes work well.

In a large saucepan on medium heat, add tomatoes, peppers, and vinegar. Bring to a simmer for 30 minutes. Blend until smooth with an immersion blender or in a food processor in batches. If blended in food processor, return to pan.

Reduce heat to low and add salt, mustard, allspice, cloves, honey, and tomato paste. Simmer uncovered for 2 hours, until it reaches desired thickness.

Autumn

The Circle of Life

Earth's eco-systems are remarkably self-contained. Things grow, things die. And all those things—plants, animals, protozoa—are deposited into the soil to fuel the next cycle. Grow, eat, poop, die. Not pretty, but that's how things work.

Humans are the only creatures on the planet that seek to interfere with the natural way of things. We grow things in the soil, eat them, and deposit the nutrient-rich waste in landfills and toilets, robbing the soil of its natural return. Without those nutrients the soil grows poor, and we are forced to find new sources of nutrients to return to the soil. Too often those fertilizers are finite resources mined from another part of the earth or derived from petrochemicals.

Composting is one way to at least partly fix that broken cycle, and autumn is when we close the loop. Organic farmers do a lot of composting, creating complete systems that enhance soil and minimize the need to bring in nutrients from the outside. Energy and nutrients that leave the farm—or your home garden—as food have to be replaced as inputs to production.

I have three composting areas and five heaps in all. A plastic standup model designed for suburban backyards takes all our kitchen peelings. A sunny corner near the garden is home to a single heap that I feed leafy garden trim. A shadier corner of the yard hosts a three-heap system where I deposit mixed grass clippings and shredded leaves from my lawn, chopped up stalks and root balls from the main garden, and whatever fallen leaves and herbivore manure I can acquire in the neighborhood.

The standup bin gets emptied once a year and produces rich, black compost, enough for a small front-yard vegetable garden. It's close to the kitchen, so it's no bother to feed. Every home should have someplace to compost organic kitchen waste; it really is a crime to throw it away. And that's no exaggeration; some regions have banned food waste from the waste stream altogether.

I like large open compost heaps because I can really see what is going on inside. I can't help but peek, poke, prod, and intervene when I get bored. It's completely okay to check inside your compost heaps. Every time you do, you introduce oxygen that will assist in the process of decomposition.

In the three-heap system, the first heap takes the raw, chunky garden waste—leaves and grass in the late summer and early fall. In the spring, I shovel that material onto the second heap,

aerating it in the process. Six months later, I move all that material to the third heap—aerating it again—where it remains until spring. At the end of eighteen months, I have a dark, homogeneous humus, which is rich finished compost.

The recipe for good compost is simple: Mix browns and greens, moisten, and stand back. Browns include fallen leaves and sun-dried weeds and garden trim. Greens consist of grass clippings, wet vegetable trim from the kitchen, and plant stalks and fresh foliage from the garden. Cut up your summer garden waste, stalks, leaves, and root balls and let them dry on the driveway or on a tarp. Save shredded leaves and grass clippings. Situate your compost in a shady corner of the yard. Put down a tarp to discourage roots from growing into the heap. A single heap will require a space about 5 ft wide and 5 ft deep (1.5 by 1.5 m). Three heaps require a space almost 20 ft (6 m) wide by 5 ft (1.5 m) deep.

Building a compost heap on a wooden shipping pallet helps aerate the heap from below.

In the fall, use your mower to pick up the leaves on the lawn, shredding the leaves and mixing them with green grass in one easy step. That instant mix of green and brown can go directly onto the compost. If you don't have a lawn mower, pull on your gardening gloves, rake the leaves, and break them up with your hands as finely as possible. It helps if they are really dry.

Avoid using cedar and juniper duff or laurel leaves in your compost as they retard microbial action.

To build the heap, lay down a base of fine, twiggy garden trim. Use oregano stems, dried pea vines, oat straw, and dried asparagus ferns to create some air space, then alternate layers of fresh and dried garden waste with layers of mixed grass clippings and shredded brown leaves. Moisten the pile with a fine spray from the hose as you build layers. Dust every second layer with ½ cup (125 mL) Basic Fertilizer Mix (p. 14) to accelerate microbial action. Every second or third layer, throw on a spade full of mature compost from another heap or rich garden soil. Include as many worms as you can find. This inoculates the heap with the bacteria and other microbes that will quickly break down plant waste, plus it introduces our friend the earthworm to a whacking great food supply.

Every couple of months, take a garden fork and fluff up the pile, moving some material from the bottom to the top and the stuff on top to the bottom. When the wet season starts, place a tarp or a piece of plastic on top to prevent rain from washing all your nutrients away. While the pile should be moist, a sodden pile will not properly decay. If you are composting in a single heap, turn the pile over whenever you get bored. The more often you aerate, the quicker and more completely the pile decomposes.

You've probably read about aerobic composting and vermicomposting, but in my experience it's not necessary to separate the two in a backyard garden. My method employs both and allows nature to take its natural course.

Layers of fresh grass clippings will mat down and turn into a slimy anaerobic mass in your compost. Mix fresh grass with brown leaves to keep the compost heap properly aerated.

For my apartment-dwelling friends: Conventional composting is not likely to be a good match for your urban lifestyle. Even one person produces too much food waste to comfortably compost under the sink (it can start to smell quite quickly) or on a balcony without help. Enter the lowly worm. Vermicomposting is the best solution for small-space applications, and worms usually work fast, consuming your scraps before they decay. Garden centers and larger seed suppliers sell self-contained vermicomposting kits, an option I strongly recommend. The resulting worm castings are a rich and nutritious medium for plant growth.

PUT THE GARDEN TO BED

Nature abhors an empty space. Any ground in your garden that isn't covered with plants or a layer of mulch is an open invitation to weeds. You should plant or mulch every square inch of garden or risk an outbreak of unwanted invasive visitors.

Set aside a part of the garden for your earliest spring crops, the vegetables you will plant before it is warm enough to work the soil, such as peas, spinach, and broad beans. Cover this area with a 6-in (15-cm) layer of shredded leaves. In the spring, just brush the leaves aside, and you are ready to plant.

Mulch protects the soil by absorbing some of the rain as it falls, preventing it from washing the nutrients out of the soil. As the leaves break down, they also create a beneficial environment—as well as a handy food source—for earthworms. Earthworm castings are a great source of nutrients for plants, and earthworm tunnels help create excellent soil structure. I harvest fall leaves from a nearby park and even rake my neighbor's leaves and haul them back to my yard. You just can't have too many leaves.

If your local climate allows it, set aside some garden space for hardy winter vegetables such as parsley, Swiss chard, kale, and leeks. Seedlings established in the first days of fall may well overwinter and provide an early harvest in spring.

The balance of the garden should be planted in late autumn with a cover crop to maintain soil structure, preserve nutrients, and increase the amount of organic material in your soil. Legumes, such as clover and field peas, are particularly effective for improving sandy and clay-rich soils and deliver an extra punch of nitrogen. White clover is a potent nitrogen fixer and creates a thick root mass near the surface of the soil that encourages soil aeration when it decays. I have also used white clover in my garden paths during the summer to suppress weeds. (Make sure your paths are wide enough to bring in the lawn mower once a month.) Crimson clover sends roots 4–5 ft (1.2–1.5 m) deep in the soil—literally dragging nutrients closer to the surface—and it puts on 2 ft (61 cm) of lush growth above the soil in spring for a big hit of green manure.

Cereal grasses bring something a little different to the party. Fall rye usually survives even harsh winter weather and is widely used on commercial farms as a soil conditioner. It is popular with home gardeners but requires tilling.

Oats deliver a larger payoff in organic material and are usually killed off during the winter by a hard frost. If you don't intend to till in the spring—or ever, if you use a no-till system—the oats will be mostly dead and decaying by the time you show up to hoe them in. Clovers and hardy grasses, such as fall rye, are much harder to kill in a no-till system. The leftover oat straw is useful to keep the soil loose and aerated on your potato patch the following spring, so I always plant it where I expect to seed potatoes the following year. My native soil is so poor and sandy that I use a combination of fall rye, crimson clover, and field legumes—so all my bases are covered. Many garden centers sell similar seed mixes for cover cropping.

Once the summer vegetables are removed from the garden, broadcast cover crop seeds by hand, according to the seed seller's directions. Gently raking the seeds into the surface of the soil will improve germination and discourage the local bird population from eating them before they sprout.

HOW TO GROW LEEKS

Leeks are a mild member of the onion family and make a fabulous flavor base for stews and soups. Growing leeks takes time, patience, and nurturing, but the payoff is substantial.

Sow leeks thickly in 4-inch pots in July, and by September they will be about 10 in (25 cm) tall and ready to transplant. The trick to getting a really good leek for cooking is to ensure that at least 6 in (15 cm) of the plant is underground to encourage a long white root. Because the roots of the plant will be well below the surface, you need to prepare the soil deeply.

Construct a simple garden box by nailing together four 3-ft (1-m) lengths of 2 x 6 lumber in a square. Remove the top 3 in (8 cm) of soil from a garden bed slightly larger than your frame and place it in a wheelbarrow. Sprinkle 4 cups (1 L) Basic Fertilizer Mix (p. 14) evenly over the bed. Place the wood frame on the bed and add 2 gal (8 L) finished compost. Mix the compost and fertilizer into the soil with a hoe.

Mix the soil in the wheelbarrow with an equal amount of compost and use it to fill the frame. To plant the leeks, remove the entire block of potting soil from the nursery container. The roots of the leek seedlings will be intertwined. Separate the leeks by gently shaking and pulling the roots apart. Dip the root mass into a bucket of water to wash away some of the soil, if they are resisting separation. Make sure the roots don't dry out while you are transplanting.

To plant the seedlings, push a trowel straight down into the soil, about 7 in (18 cm) deep. Push the soil to the side to create a gap and slide the leek down into the space you created behind the trowel, about 6 in (15 cm) deep. Slide the trowel straight up from the hole and let the soil fall loosely around the stalk of the plant. Plant the

seedlings about 6 in (15 cm) apart. When all the leeks are planted, use a watering can to mud the entire bed.

As the compost in your soil mixture breaks down over the next couple of months, it will make room for the expanding girth of your leeks. The compost also adds protection against the bed drying out, acting as mulch.

HOME CANNING BASICS

Home canning is immensely rewarding and relatively simple once you grasp the essentials. Near the end of the growing season, many home gardeners are inundated with fresh produce, far more than they can eat fresh. Canning is an effective way to preserve the bounty for the leaner months ahead.

The environment is full of yeasts, molds, and bacteria that promote decay. To preserve foods, you must create a sealed environment, free of pathogens. Heat processing raises the temperature inside a sealed container enough to ensure that all such micro-organisms are destroyed. Home-canning kits can be purchased at many hardware and home stores. If you are a novice, I strongly recommend that you buy a complete kit rather than trying to assemble the gear yourself and risk having the wrong tools for the job.

A home canning outfit should include:

- a large, deep pot and a fitted metal rack with handles to raise and lower the jars

- long rubber-lined jar-lifting tongs for handling hot jars

- a canning funnel to keep jar edges clean

- a ladle, metal tongs, and a long-handled spoon

- Mason jars with fitted snap lids and sealing rings

Ensure the jars are clean, then immerse them in boiling water until needed. Place lids, rings, metal tongs, and ladle in a large bowl and cover with boiling water from the kettle. Remove them with another set of tongs as needed.

Set up a workflow with an area for filling jars next to the stove and a space lined with tea towels on the other side of the stove for resting jars after they are processed.

Use the funnel and a ladle to pour foods into the jars to keep jar edges as clean as possible. Use a long-handled spoon to push food down from the top of the jar (creating the "headspace," the distance between the top of the contents and the edge of the jar) before removing the funnel. Use a clean cloth to wipe off any residue from the jar edges.

Place a sterile lid on each full jar using tongs, and seal, finger-tight, with a ring. Place the jars on the rack and lower into boiling water for the time prescribed by the recipe. The tops of the jars should be at least 1 in (2.5 cm) below the surface of the water. Top up with boiling water from the kettle, if necessary. Remove the processed jars with a jar lifter and move to the resting station.

As the jars cool, the lids should snap down with reverse pressure. Lids that do not snap down are not properly sealed and should not be stored for long periods. It is safest to let them finish cooling and then store in the refrigerator for short-term consumption.

Processing times and headspace vary by jar size and contents.

 Normal heat processing is used for foods with high acidity, such as pickles, relishes, and fruit jams. Low-acid foods, such as unbrined vegetables and meats, require pressure canning to achieve an internal temperature of 240°F (116°C).

Most modern varieties of tomatoes are too low in acidity to be safely canned without the addition of lemon juice or vinegar.

Old-Fashioned Bread & Butter Pickles

This is an old but ageless family recipe.
I love these pickles on hot dogs, beside a sandwich, in a box, and with a fox.

MAKES 6 PINT (500-ML) JARS

4 lb (1.8 kg) field cucumbers

2 Spanish onions

¼ cup (60 mL) coarse pickling salt

48 ice cubes

2 cups (500 mL) apple cider vinegar

½ cup (125 mL) white vinegar

3 cups (750 mL) sugar

2 tbsp mustard seeds

1 tbsp celery seeds

1 tsp ground turmeric

¼ tsp ground cloves

1 roasted red bell pepper (p. 45)

Scrub cucumbers clean and slice ¼-in (6-mm) thick. Peel and cut onions in half and slice as thinly as possible. Toss cucumbers and onions in a large bowl with pickling salt and 24 ice cubes. Place remaining ice cubes over top of mix and let stand for 3 hours. Immerse mixture in fresh cold water twice and set aside to drain.

Immerse 6 pint (500-mL) canning jars with lids and rings in boiling water. Remove from water as needed.

In a large pot on high heat, combine vinegar, sugar, mustard and celery seeds, turmeric, and cloves. Bring to a boil. Roughly chop roasted red pepper and add to pot along with cucumbers and onions. Reduce heat to low and simmer for 5 minutes. Ladle hot mixture into jars, leaving ½-in (1-cm) headspace.

Cover with a sterilized lid and seal, finger-tight, with a ring. Process jars in boiling water for 10 minutes. Set aside to cool.

Classic Dill Pickles

Home preserving is making a huge comeback and there is no easier place to start than a nice low-risk dill pickle. Even people in Neolithic times successfully pickled food, so there's no reason you can't do it.

MAKES 6 1 QT/L JARS

5 lb (2.2 kg) pickling cucumbers

3 cups (750 mL) white vinegar

1 cup (250 mL) coarse pickling salt

6 large sprigs dill weed

6 garlic cloves

Safety Note: This is an old family recipe that does not call for heat processing. However, many modern recipes direct you to submerge freshly filled jars in boiling water after sealing. If you choose this route, leave ½-in (1-cm) headspace at top of jar before you seal it. Immerse jars in boiling water bath for 10 minutes.

Thoroughly scrub cucumbers under cold running water. In a large pot on high heat, bring 10 cups (2.5 L) water, vinegar, and salt to a boil.

In a second pot of boiling water, place 6 1qt/L Mason jars, lids, and rings. Remove as required and place 1 sprig dill weed and 1 garlic clove in bottom of each jar. Tilt jar toward you and place cucumbers vertically in jar. Use smaller cucumbers to fill gaps at top of jar. Pour boiling brine into jars and fill to top. Cover with a sterilized lid and seal, finger-tight, with a ring. Set aside to cool.

Old-Fashioned Relish

Commercially prepared relish often contains starch from genetically engineered corn, high-fructose corn syrup, sodium benzoate, potassium sorbate, xantham gum, polysorbate 80, and sulfites. I prefer condiments made from natural ingredients. We serve this relish at our summer barbecue parties and always end up giving people jars to take home. It's that good.

MAKES 8 PINT (500-ML) JARS

4 cups (1 L) ground cucumbers

4 cups (1 L) ground celery

4 cups (1 L) ground onions

2 green bell peppers, ground

1 red bell pepper, ground

⅔ cup (160 mL) pickling salt

4 cups (1 L) sugar

2¾ cups (685 mL) white vinegar

1 tsp ground turmeric

1 tsp curry powder

1 tbsp mustard seeds

1 tbsp celery seeds

¾ cup (185 mL) all purpose flour

1¼ cups (310 mL) white vinegar

Grind vegetables in a meat grinder or use the pulse button of a food processor.

Place ground vegetables in a large, non-reactive (glass, ceramic, or stainless steel) bowl and stir in pickling salt. Refrigerate overnight. Rinse mixture with cold water and squeeze out moisture.

In a large pot on high heat, combine sugar and 2¾ cups (685 mL) white vinegar. Add turmeric, curry powder, and mustard and celery seeds. Bring to a boil. Add ground vegetables and simmer for 10 minutes.

In a bowl, whisk flour with 1¼ cups (310 mL) vinegar. While stirring briskly, add to vegetable mixture. Cook for 15 minutes.

Ladle mixture into sterilized pint (500-mL) jars, leaving ¼-in (6-mm) headspace. Cover with a sterilized lid and seal, finger-tight, with a ring. Immerse jars in boiling water and process for 10 minutes. Remove and set aside to cool.

Spicy Pickled Beets

I have a life-long love affair with pickled beets, which were always a sweet, tangy staple on the table at Nana's house. These spicy pickles will keep for several years.

4 lb (1.8 kg) red beets

2 cups (500 mL) white vinegar

1 cup (250 mL) white sugar

1 tsp coarse salt

12 whole cloves

12 allspice berries

In a large pot of boiling water, simmer whole, unpeeled beets until knife-tender, at least 20–30 minutes. Remove and let cool for 5 minutes.

In a separate pot, boil 1 cup (250 mL) water, vinegar, sugar, and salt. Add 3 whole cloves and 3 allspice berries to each jar. Slice beets to desired thickness (⅛–¼ in [3–6 mm]) and pack tightly in sterilized pint (500-mL) canning jars. Ladle boiling hot pickling liquid over beets, leaving ½-in (1-cm) headspace. Cover with a sterilized lid and seal, finger-tight, with a ring. Immerse jars in boiling water for 10 minutes. Remove and set aside to cool.

Even Easier Pickled Beets

No special equipment or processing is needed for this refrigerator version of pickled beets, but they don't keep forever. Plan to give some away. Use a long beet, such as Cylindra, Taunus, or Rodina for a uniform-sized pickle.

MAKES 8 CUPS (2 L)

3 lb (1.5 kg) beets	1 tbsp ground cinnamon
2 cups (500 mL) apple cider vinegar	1 tsp ground allspice
1¾ cups (415 mL) white sugar	10 whole cloves

In a large pot on high heat, boil whole, unpeeled beets in water until knife-tender, about 25 minutes. Drain and cover with cold water. Set aside until cool. With a sharp knife, peel beets and remove stems and roots. Slice into ¼-in (6-mm) rounds.

In a large saucepan on high heat, combine vinegar, 2 cups (500 mL) water, sugar, cinnamon, allspice, and cloves. Bring to a boil and simmer for 3 minutes. Add beets and simmer for 15 minutes. Remove and set aside to cool. Place beets and liquid in clean jars. Seal with clean lids and keep refrigerated. Will keep for up to 1 month.

Farm-Style Pear Sauce

In my neighborhood, you either pick your pears early or a 400-lb black bear does it for you. Recently, Boo-boo got every single pear from two of my trees and left me with a bunch of mangled branches. The following season, I was ready for him. I picked every pear at the end of August. While some of the fruit ripens readily, some may remain persistently green. No matter; when you make pear sauce, you can use a mix of ripe and firm fruit. I let the kids stir this pear sauce into their yogurt or dollop it on pork chops. Pear sauce can also be substituted for apple sauce in sweet loaf cakes.

MAKES 4–5 ½-PINT (250-ML) JARS

4 lb (1.8 kg) Bosc pears, peeled, cored, and sliced

1 tbsp lemon juice

1 tsp ground cinnamon

2 tbsp brown sugar (optional)

In a large saucepan on medium high heat, combine pear slices, lemon juice, and ¼ cup (60 mL) water and bring to a boil. Reduce heat and simmer for 15 minutes. Stir in cinnamon and, if you wish, sugar. Taste and adjust for sweetness, adding sugar 1 tbsp at a time. For a smooth sauce, blend in a food processor or with an immersion blender.

Freeze in plastic tubs or preserve in jars, with a home canning rig.

To can pear sauce, ladle into ½-pint (250-mL) jars, leaving ½-in (1-cm) headspace. Wipe rims clean. Cover with a sterilized lid and seal, finger-tight, with a ring. Immerse jars in boiling water for 10 minutes. Remove and set aside to cool.

Garden Harvest Minestrone

Minestrone is the perfect soup for harvest season, when all the ingredients are ready to pick at the same time. I'm certain that is how the traditional recipe was invented. Why fool with perfection? These flavors make sense together.

MAKES 6 SERVINGS

2 tbsp extra virgin olive oil

2 oz (60 g) pancetta, cut into ¼-in (6-mm) strips

1 cup (250 mL) diced onions

2 celery stalks, halved and chopped

1 cup (250 mL) diced carrots

2 garlic cloves, minced

1½ cups (355 mL) diced zucchini

2 cups (500 mL) chopped lacinato kale

1 28-oz (796-mL) can plum tomatoes

2 cups (500 mL) Homemade (p. 176) or low-sodium chicken stock

½ cup (125 mL) white wine

¼ tsp ground black pepper

1 Parmesan cheese rind (optional)

½ cup (125 mL) dried macaroni

1 14-oz (398-mL) can cannellini beans, drained and washed

2 tbsp chopped fresh fennel fronds

¼ cup (60 mL) finely grated Parmesan cheese

12 fresh basil leaves

Canned tomatoes, bacon, cheese, and stock may all contain salt, but in amounts that differ by brand. You will need to taste your soup at the end of the cooking process and season it to taste.

In a large saucepan on medium, heat olive oil. Add pancetta and sauté, stirring occasionally, until crisp. Add onions, celery, carrots, and garlic, and sauté until softened, about 10 minutes. Add zucchini and kale. Break up whole tomatoes with your fingers before adding to pan.

Add stock, wine, pepper, and cheese rind. Simmer for 10 minutes. Taste and season with salt, if desired. Add macaroni and beans and simmer for 15 minutes. Remove and discard cheese rind. Stir in fennel fronds. Garnish bowls with cheese and basil leaves.

Clockwise from top: Roasted Tomato Basil Soup (p. 140), Cheddar Dill Biscuits (p. 163), African-style Butternut Squash Soup (opposite)

African-Style Butternut Squash Soup

Harissa is a fiery condiment made from red bell peppers, chilies, and a variety of spices that originate in North Africa. It helps temper the natural sweetness of the squash.

MAKES 6 SERVINGS

3 lb (1.5 kg) butternut squash

2½ tsp kosher salt, divided

1½ tbsp olive oil, divided

2 cups (500 mL) diced onions

1 head roasted garlic (p. 141)

3 cups (750 mL) low-sodium chicken or vegetable stock

1–2 tsp harissa paste, to taste

6 tbsp sour cream

cilantro, for garnish

Preheat oven to 350°F (180°C).

Split squash and remove seeds. Place halves skin side down on a baking sheet and season with ½ tsp salt and ½ tbsp olive oil. Bake for 1 hour, until tender. Set aside to cool, then remove flesh with a spoon.

In a large saucepan on medium, heat remainder of oil. Sauté onions until lightly browned, about 5 minutes.

Add squash, roasted garlic, stock, harissa, and remainder of salt. Bring to a boil, then reduce heat to low and simmer for 30 minutes. Blend until smooth with an immersion blender or in an upright blender or food processor. Garnish each bowl with 1 tbsp sour cream and a few cilantro leaves.

Roasted Tomato Basil Soup

Delicately nuanced, with natural sugars and aromatic basil, this tomato soup cannot be beat. Roasting caramelizes and mellows the tomatoes and garlic.

MAKES 4 SERVINGS

2 lb (1 kg) plum-sized tomatoes, halved

2 garlic cloves, minced

1½ tsp kosher salt, divided

1½ tsp cracked black pepper, divided

3 tbsp olive oil, divided

½ cup (125 mL) diced onions

¼ cup (60 mL) minced shallots

½ cup (125 mL) cream

½ cup (125 mL) milk

½ cup (125 mL) low-sodium chicken or vegetable stock

¼ cup (60 mL) chopped basil leaves

3 tbsp sour cream

1 tbsp milk

1 tbsp minced basil leaves

Place about 10–12 plum-sized tomatoes (roughly 2 lb [1 kg]) onto a cookie sheet and freeze. When they're frozen solid, throw them into a ziplock bag to store in the freezer. Now you have your own garden-grown tomatoes to add to soups, stews, and sauces all winter long.

I grow San Marzano tomatoes for sauces because of the high ratio of flesh to seeds. Amish Paste and Roma are also good choices. It takes about 6 plum-sized tomatoes to make up a pound (500 g).

Preheat oven to 300°F (150°C).

In a large roasting pan, place halved tomatoes cut side up. Sprinkle with garlic, ½ tsp salt, and ½ tsp pepper, and drizzle with 2 tbsp olive oil. Bake for 2 hours.

In a large pot on medium-low, heat 1 tbsp olive oil. Sauté onions and shallots until soft, about 5 minutes. Add roasted tomatoes and pan juices and mash with a spoon. Add cream, milk, stock, remainder of salt and pepper, and ¼ cup (60 mL) basil and cook for about 5 minutes. Blend until smooth with an immersion blender, or in an upright blender or food processor.

In a small bowl, combine sour cream, 1 tbsp milk, and minced basil. Ladle soup into bowls and garnish with sour cream mixture.

Roasted Garlic

Pungent garlic takes on a nutty sweetness when roasted. It's the perfect way to flavor soups and mashed potatoes, as a condiment with grilled meats, or simply spread on a cracker. I make up to 6 at a time.

1 head garlic
⅛ tsp kosher salt
¼ tsp extra virgin olive oil

Preheat oven to 350°F (180°C).

Cut top ¼ in (6 mm) from garlic bulb to expose inside of each clove. Place head on a sheet of foil. Season top with salt and olive oil, wrap foil over to seal, and roast for 50–60 minutes.

Darcy's Onion Soup

French onion soup is a bit of a dusty classic. Popular in the '60s and '70s, it was done so widely and so badly that it became a bit of a joke. But done well, really deep flavors emerge from the cooking process, the kind you will never get from a packet or tin. Forget French onion soup—this is how we do onion soup in Canada. (Actually, it's how my wife does it.)

MAKES 4 SERVINGS

3 Spanish onions

3 shallots

5 medium leeks

1 tbsp extra virgin olive oil

1 tbsp butter

2 garlic cloves, chopped

2 tsp fresh thyme leaves

4 cups (1 L) Homemade (p. 176) or low-sodium chicken stock

1 tsp sea salt

¼ tsp ground black pepper

4 slices French bread

1 cup (250 mL) grated Gruyère or white cheddar cheese

fresh thyme leaves, for garnish

Peel, halve, and thinly slice onions and shallots. Split and rinse leeks to remove grit, then thinly slice white stalks (don't use green tops and roots).

In a large saucepan on medium, heat olive oil and butter. Sauté onions, shallots, and leeks, stirring about once a minute, until they turn golden brown and volume reduces by about two-thirds. Add garlic and thyme and sauté for another 2 minutes. Add chicken stock and simmer for 10 minutes. Season soup to taste with salt and pepper.

Preheat broiler to high. Ladle soup into 4 oven-proof bowls. Toast bread and place on top of each bowl. Sprinkle ¼ cup (60 mL) grated cheese on top of each slice. Place under broiler for about 4–8 minutes, until golden brown and bubbling. Garnish with a sprinkle of fresh thyme leaves.

Baked Chicken & Rice
(Arroz con Pollo)

Gone are the days when accomplished cooks and professional chefs felt that to make "authentic" Italian or Spanish food, the ingredients had to come from Italy or Spain. Even a few years ago, local prosciutto and serrano-style ham couldn't hold a candle to the real thing. That has changed. Make this dish with the terroir of your surroundings, using local and home-grown ingredients. Your Arroz con Pollo can be of this place, not that one. Do this, and you can forgive yourself a little tub of imported green olives from Spain. Think of it as a tip of your hat to the country that invented the dish.

MAKES 4–6 SERVINGS

1 tbsp canola oil

4 oz (115 g) bacon or Serrano-style ham, cut into ¼-in (6-mm) strips

1 3–4-lb (1.4–1.8-kg) fryer chicken, cut into pieces

1 tsp kosher salt

½ tsp ground black pepper

2 tsp smoked paprika

2 cups (500 mL) diced onions

3 garlic cloves, chopped

2 cups (500 mL) basmati rice

3 cups (750 mL) low-sodium chicken stock

1 cup (250 mL) peas or blanched green beans

½ cup (125 mL) diced roasted red pepper (p. 45)

¼ cup (60 mL) pitted, chopped green olives

Preheat oven to 300°F (150°C).

In a heavy-bottomed pan on medium, heat canola oil. Add bacon and sauté until crisp. Remove bacon and set aside. Season chicken pieces with salt, pepper, and paprika. Add to pan and brown for 5 minutes on each side. Remove chicken and set aside. Sauté onions and garlic for about 5 minutes, until golden. Add rice and stir until coated with oil. Increase heat to medium-high and pour in stock. Return chicken to pan, and bring to a low boil for 10 minutes. Taste and season with additional salt, if desired. Cover pot with tight-fitting lid and bake for 30 minutes. Stir in peas or beans, roasted peppers, and olives. Cover with lid and let sit for 5 minutes. Sprinkle bacon over top and serve.

Lamb & Spinach Kebabs

Fresh spinach adds moisture and tenderness to this Middle Eastern favorite. Sunflower seeds add a little crunch. Kebabs are happiest wrapped in warm, fresh pita bread. Serve with Salsa Verde (p. 30) and Super Simple Pita Bread (p. 62).

MAKES 6 SERVINGS

1 lb (500 mL) ground lamb

1 garlic clove, minced

½ tsp ground cumin

½ tsp ground black pepper

1 tsp kosher salt

1 egg, lightly beaten

½ cup (125 mL) chopped spinach

¼ cup (60 mL) sunflower seeds

3 tbsp plain bread crumbs

In my recipes, you can substitute arugula for spinach to add a grown-up hint of bitterness and peppery bite.

Soak 6 bamboo skewers in water for 30 minutes.

In a large mixing bowl, mix all ingredients. Knead with your hands until mixture firms up. Form mixture into balls about the size of a small mandarin orange, and then roll into a tube shape and run a skewer through it lengthwise. Refrigerate for 30 minutes.

Preheat barbecue to high. Coat grill with canola oil to prevent sticking. Grill kebabs for about 3 minutes before turning them. (They may stick if you don't allow the meat to brown and form a crust where it is in contact with the grill.) After 3 minutes, turn every 1–2 minutes until kebabs are browned and firm to the touch, about 7–8 minutes.

Lamb Shoulder Chops with Coriander Rub

Cilantro routinely bolts in the heat of summer, creating tough seedy tops rather than lush green foliage, but this coriander-rubbed lamb shoulder made from the seeds is a proverbial silver lining in that cloud. Serve with Chickpeas in Cilantro Pesto (p. 34).

MAKES 4 SERVINGS; CORIANDER RUB MAKES ¼ CUP (60 ML)

¼ cup (60 mL) Coriander Rub (see sidebar)

2 tbsp extra virgin olive oil

4 8-oz (230-g) lamb shoulder chops

¼ cup (60 mL) cilantro leaves

1 lemon, cut into wedges

CORIANDER RUB:

2 tbsp coriander seeds

1 tbsp cumin seeds

2 tsp whole black peppercorns

2 tsp kosher salt

Preheat oven to 350°F (180°C).

In a small bowl, combine Coriander Rub with olive oil and rub on lamb chops. Set aside for 1 hour.

In a cast-iron frying pan on medium-high heat, sear lamb chops for 2 minutes on each side. Place frying pan and chops in oven and bake for 5 minutes. Remove from oven and cover with foil for 5 minutes, then sprinkle with cilantro leaves and squeeze lemon wedges over top.

CORIANDER RUB:

In a dry frying pan on medium heat, toast coriander and cumin seeds and peppercorns until fragrant, about 3 minutes. Grind toasted spices in a mortar and pestle or spice grinder. Combine with salt.

African Lamb Shanks

Peanuts and chilies give this dish a subtle but exotic twist. Don't be intimidated by the long list of ingredients; most of this stuff is already sitting around in your pantry. Use a big oven-proof pot with a tight-fitting lid. The long cooking time ensures tender meat and rich, well-developed flavors. Substitute black peppercorns if you can't find Indonesian long pepper.

MAKES 4 SERVINGS

4 lamb shanks

2 tsp kosher salt, divided

1 tsp ground Indonesian long pepper, divided

3 tbsp olive oil

1 cup (250 mL) diced celery

1 cup (250 mL) diced onions

2 green onions, chopped

3 carrots, roughly chopped

1 garlic clove, chopped

1 red bell pepper, diced

1 dried red chili pepper, crumbled

1 tsp ground cumin

1 tsp smoked hot paprika

½ cup (125 mL) white wine

3 tbsp peanut butter

1½ cups (375 mL) low-sodium chicken or veal stock

¼ cup (60 mL) chopped peanuts

2 tbsp cilantro leaves

Preheat oven to 250°F (120°C).

Rub shanks with 1 tsp salt and ½ tsp pepper. In a heavy-bottomed pot on medium, heat olive oil. Sear shanks for about 5 minutes on each surface. Remove shanks and set aside. Add celery, onions, carrots, garlic, and bell peppers and sauté until softened, about 5 minutes. Add chili, cumin, paprika, and remainder of salt and pepper and stir until fragrant. Increase heat to medium-high, add white wine, and bring to a boil to evaporate alcohol. Stir in peanut butter until well combined, then add stock. Return lamb shanks to pot and work them down until mostly covered. Cover pot with lid and bake for 2 hours. Turn shanks over and bake for 1 more hour. Garnish with chopped peanuts and cilantro leaves.

Left: Bacon & Mushroom Kale (p. 160)
Right: African Lamb Shanks (opposite)

Herbed Mustard Rack of Lamb

You and your partner can share a rack of lamb for less than the price of two steaks, and it's a much more romantic dish. Spring this one on your spouse for home date night with a bottle of red wine. Serve alongside Green Beans with Pepitas (p. 158).

MAKES 2 SERVINGS

1 8-bone rack of lamb

¼ tsp fine sea salt

1 tsp fresh thyme leaves

1 tbsp fresh rosemary leaves

¼ tsp kosher salt

10 whole black peppercorns

1 tbsp extra virgin olive oil

½ tsp whole grain mustard

1 tsp Dijon mustard

How to remove silver skin: Loins and primal cuts of meat often have a sheet of tough, chewy connective tissue on the outside of the muscle that must be removed before cooking. Using a very sharp, thin-bladed knife, slide tip under silver skin about 1 in (2.5 cm) from edge and cut outward to create a flat ribbon. Use a small piece of paper towel to grip silver skin. Turn knife blade back toward uncut silver skin. Glide knife between skin and meat, keeping blade of knife flat and flush with skin. Use long, gentle strokes as you cut.

Remove lamb from refrigerator 1 hour before cooking to warm to room temperature. Remove silver skin (see sidebar) and season with sea salt. Cover and set aside.

Preheat oven to 425°F (220°C).

Roughly chop thyme and rosemary and place in a mortar with kosher salt and peppercorns. Grind until fine. (Salt acts as an abrasive to help break down herbs). In a bowl, combine olive oil, herb mixture, and mustards.

Warm an oven-safe frying pan on medium-high heat. Cook lamb rack meat-side down for 3 minutes, until browned. Turn rack over and sear bottom for 2 minutes. Smear herb glaze over meat and bake in frying pan for 10 minutes, or until internal temperature of meat reaches 125°F (52°C). Cover with foil and set aside for 10 minutes. Slice between bones to make chops.

Grilled Lamb with Herbs

Cooking a bone-in leg of lamb to a desirable and uniform doneness is very difficult, but grilling a deboned leg is a breeze, and far more surface area comes in contact with the herbs and seasoning. If you like the flavorful, crunchy edges on grilled meat, you are going to love this lamb. Serve with Chimichurri (p. 29) and Grilled Autumn Vegetables (p. 159).

MAKES 6 SERVINGS

1 leg of lamb, deboned and flattened for grilling

1 tbsp fresh thyme leaves

1 tbsp fresh rosemary leaves

¼ cup (60 mL) chopped chives

6 garlic cloves, smashed

4 tbsp olive oil

½ tsp ground black pepper

1 tsp coarse sea salt

2 8-in (20-cm) sprigs rosemary

Chef trick: To ensure meat is properly cooked, always check internal temperature rather than cooking time.

Place lamb in a large glass or ceramic baking dish. In a bowl, combine thyme, rosemary, chives, garlic, olive oil, pepper, and salt and mash to bruise herbs and draw out flavorful oils. Rub herb mixture on lamb. Cover with beeswax wrap or cling film and marinate for at least 2 hours.

Preheat barbecue to high. Place rosemary sprigs on grill and place lamb on rosemary. Grill for about 6 minutes. Turn lamb and grill for another 5 minutes. Reduce heat to low and grill until internal temperature of meat reaches 130°F (55°C). Remove lamb from grill, place on a plate, and cover with foil. Let sit for 10 minutes, then slice off pieces about ½-in (1-cm) thick across grain of meat.

French Lentil Stew with Lamb Sausages

Lentils are a decidedly unsexy ingredient, but they are one of the healthiest foods you can eat and a sustainable source of protein. Need more fiber? Controlling cholesterol? Lentils are your friend. If you are cutting back on meat, leave out the sausage.

MAKES 4 SERVINGS

1 ½ cups (375 mL) Puy lentils

2 cups (500 mL) water

¼ cup (60 mL) extra virgin olive oil

1 lb (500 g) lamb sausages

¾ cup (185 mL) diced red onions

1 cup (250 mL) diced carrots

½ cup (125 mL) diced celery

2 garlic cloves, minced

2 tbsp fresh rosemary leaves

1 tsp kosher salt

½ tsp ground black pepper

1 cup (250 mL) low-sodium chicken stock

1 cup (250 mL) Fresh Sofrito (p. 82)

To avoid toughening the skin of dried legumes, cook lentils, chickpeas, and beans until tender before seasoning with salt.

Puy or French green lentils are shaped like small, black flying saucers and take fresh herb flavors like a champ.

Wash lentils in cold water, rinsing 3 or 4 times, to remove surface starch. In a saucepan on high heat, bring lentils to a boil in water, then reduce heat to low and simmer uncovered for about 30 minutes, or until tender. Add more water if needed. Drain and set aside.

In a large pot or Dutch oven on medium, heat olive oil. Add sausages and cook until browned on all sides, about 8–10 minutes. Remove sausages from pan, cut into ¼-in (6-mm) slices, and set aside. Add onions, carrots, celery, garlic, rosemary, salt, and pepper and sauté for about 5 minutes, until tender. Add cooked lentils and stock. Return sausages to pot and simmer gently to reduce liquid. Taste and season with salt, if desired. (Sometimes sausages will give up enough salt and sometimes not.) Serve in flat bowls topped with Fresh Sofrito.

Darcy's New World Bolognese Sauce

We use this to sauce penne or toss it with linguini that will be baked under a heap of grated Pecorino cheese. It also makes a fine meat sauce for lasagna. The grated vegetables, fresh herbs, and pungent spices meld to form a robust and very nutritious sauce.

MAKES 6 SERVINGS

- 1 tbsp extra virgin olive oil
- 1 lb (500 g) ground beef
- 2 hot Italian sausages, casings removed, or ½ lb (250 g) chopped Italian Sausage Meatballs (p. 50)
- 2 garlic cloves, minced
- 1 medium onion, minced
- 1 carrot, finely grated
- 6 large fresh button mushrooms, thinly sliced
- 1 medium zucchini, coarsely grated
- 1 tbsp kosher salt
- 2 tbsp fresh oregano
- 1 tbsp dried marjoram
- 2 tbsp fresh basil leaves
- 2 tsp fresh thyme leaves
- ½ tsp ground black pepper
- ½ tsp cracked red chili flakes
- 1 tbsp chopped fresh rosemary leaves
- 3 cups (750 mL) tomato sauce
- ¼ cup (60 mL) tomato paste
- 2 cups (500 mL) low-sodium beef stock

When substituting dried herbs for fresh, cut the amount by about two-thirds. Dried herbs are far stronger than fresh.

In a large pot on medium, heat olive oil. Cook ground beef and sausage meat, breaking up meat with a wooden spoon until browned, about 5 minutes. Add garlic and onions and cook until translucent. Add carrots, mushrooms, and zucchini, and cook until soft.

Add salt, oregano, marjoram, basil, thyme, pepper, chili flakes, and rosemary and cook for 2 minutes. Stir in tomato sauce, paste, and stock, reduce heat to low, and simmer, uncovered, for 1–3 hours. Taste and season with more salt, if desired.

Spicy Meatballs in Greek Tomato Sauce

It is safe to say that I have never met a meatball that I didn't like, but keftedes are meatballs that I like a great deal. These spicy little numbers are served in Greece as snacks, appetizers, and as a main course in tomato sauce. The sauce and the meatballs have a hint of subtle exotic spice, but not enough that you can tell exactly which spices are used. Only you will know. Feel free to substitute beef for some or all of the lamb. They'll be just as authentic. Serve on a bed of rice or noodles, topped with crumbled feta cheese.

MAKES 4–6 SERVINGS OR A PARTY PLATTER

SPICY MEATBALLS:

2 eggs, lightly beaten

¼ cup (60 mL) milk

2 lb (1 kg) ground lamb

2 tbsp chopped fresh oregano

4 tbsp chopped fresh flat-leaf parsley

2 cups (500 mL) bread crumbs

1 tsp ground black pepper

1 tbsp kosher salt

¼ tsp ground cinnamon

¼ tsp ground nutmeg

¼ tsp ground allspice

¾ cup (185 mL) minced leeks, white part only

3 garlic cloves, minced

½ cup (125 mL) extra virgin olive oil

GREEK TOMATO SAUCE:

2 tbsp extra virgin olive oil

1 garlic clove, chopped

3 cups (750 mL) strained canned tomatoes

¼ tsp ground cinnamon

¼ tsp ground nutmeg

¼ tsp ground allspice

sea salt, to taste

honey, to taste

½ cup (125 mL) crumbled feta cheese

SPICY MEATBALLS:

In a bowl, whisk eggs and milk together and set aside. In a large mixing bowl, break up ground lamb and mix in oregano, parsley, bread crumbs, pepper, salt, cinnamon, nutmeg, allspice, leeks, and garlic. Add egg mixture and knead lightly to combine. Roll into golf-ball-sized meatballs.

In a frying pan on medium, heat olive oil. Fry meatballs in batches—don't crowd the pan; leave about 1 in (2.5 cm) between them. Turn occasionally to brown evenly and cook about 6 minutes, until firm to the touch.

GREEK TOMATO SAUCE:

In a large saucepan on medium-low, heat olive oil. Sauté garlic until fragrant, about 1 minute, stirring regularly. Add tomatoes, cinnamon, nutmeg, and allspice and simmer for 30 minutes. Taste and season with salt and honey, if desired. (Some canned tomatoes are already salted and sweetened.) Add meatballs to sauce and simmer for 20 minutes. Top with feta cheese.

Beef & Spinach Cabbage Rolls

The standard filling for cabbage rolls is ground beef and leftover rice. My talented wife added chopped spinach that I collected from the greenhouse and fresh ground pepper for a nice, spicy finish. Feel free to use chard leaves or arugula instead.

MAKES 4–6 SERVINGS

1 large head green or savoy cabbage

1 lb (500 g) lean ground beef

1 cup (250 mL) cooked rice

1 cup (250 mL) finely chopped fresh
   spinach

1 medium onion, puréed

4 garlic cloves, minced

1 tsp kosher salt

1 tsp black pepper

1 28-oz (796-mL) tin diced tomatoes

1 15-oz (398-mL) tin tomato sauce

¼ tsp cayenne

1 tbsp chopped fresh oregano

1 tbsp chopped fresh basil

Preheat oven to 350°F (180°C).

With a sharp, thin-bladed knife, remove core from cabbage. In a large pot on high heat, bring 6 qt/L water to a boil and add cabbage, core-side up. Use tongs to remove outer leaves without tearing them as they come loose. With a knife, remove tough part of stalk from each cabbage leaf. Set aside largest, intact leaves for rolls.

In a large bowl, combine ground beef, rice, spinach, onions, garlic, salt, and pepper. In a separate bowl, combine tomatoes and sauce. Stir in cayenne, oregano, and basil.

Line a roaster with 1 layer of remaining cabbage leaves and 1 cup (250 mL) tomato mixture.

With stalk end of cabbage leaf closest to you, place about ¼–⅓ cup (60–80 mL) meat filling on leaf. Roll leaf over filling once, then fold in sides toward each other and continue to roll up leaf, away from you. Place rolls in rows in roaster and cover with remaining tomato mixture. Place remaining cabbage leaves in a layer over top and cover entire pan with a lid or foil. Bake for 90 minutes.

Baked Zucchini Ratatouille

My ratatouille recipe does not include eggplant because my wife doesn't like it, and chances are good you aren't growing it. You won't miss it. This is my riff on the French classic, one that should dovetail very nicely with what your garden provides in late summer and early fall. If you don't have pattypan squash, yellow zucchini is a nice substitute.

MAKES 6 SERVINGS

- 2 tbsp olive oil, divided
- 2 cups (500 mL) diced green zucchini
- 2 cups (500 mL) diced yellow pattypan squash
- 1 garlic clove, minced
- 1 medium onion, diced
- 1 cup (250 mL) minced tomatoes
- ½ cup diced green bell peppers
- ½ cup (125 mL) peas or diced green beans
- 2 tbsp tomato paste
- 1 tsp sea salt
- ½ tsp ground black pepper
- ½ tsp fresh thyme leaves
- 1 tbsp chopped fresh basil leaves
- 1½ cups (375 mL) grated mozzarella cheese

In my rural neighborhood, the joke is that the only time people lock their car doors is in September; walk away from an unlocked car, and you will come back to find a large zucchini inside. Only it's not a joke or some urban legend. I do this to my neighbors at least weekly during zucchini season.

Preheat oven to 350°F (180°C).

In a large flat-bottomed pan on high, heat 1 tbsp olive oil. Sauté zucchini and squash while stirring gently until brown edges appear, about 1 minute. Transfer mixture to a 10-in (25-cm) round baking dish. Return pan to stove, lower heat to medium, and add remainder of olive oil, garlic, onions, tomatoes, bell peppers, and green beans. Sauté until softened, about 3 minutes. Add tomato paste, salt, pepper, thyme, and basil and continue to cook until a thick sauce forms. Pour sauce over zucchini mixture. Sprinkle cheese evenly over dish. Bake on middle rack of oven for 15 minutes. Turn broiler to high until cheese turns a golden brown, about 1 minute—watch it closely; it will burn quickly.

Angry Penne
with Spicy Arrabiata Sauce

This Roman-style sauce with garlic and hot peppers is called arrabiata, meaning "angry." A tasty sauce is that quite rustic, it takes only about twenty minutes to prepare.

MAKES 4 SERVINGS; SAUCE MAKES 2 CUPS (500 ML)

SAUCE:

3 tbsp olive oil

4 garlic cloves, chopped

½ cup (125 mL) minced onions

2 dried hot chilies, crumbled

2 lb (1 kg) plum tomatoes, chopped

¼ cup (60 mL) red wine

1 tsp kosher salt

ANGRY PENNE:

1 lb (500 g) dried penne

2 tbsp kosher salt

2 cups (500 mL) Arrabiata Sauce

¼ cup (60 mL) chopped flat-leaf parsley

When fresh tomatoes aren't available, substitute 1 28-oz (796-mL) can diced or stewed tomatoes. If you use canned whole tomatoes, give them a rough chop or squeeze them through your fingers.

SAUCE:
In a large saucepan on medium-low, heat olive oil. Sauté garlic, onions, and chilies about 3 minutes, until onions soften. Add tomatoes, stir in wine, and increase temperature to medium. Cook at a fast simmer for 10 minutes. Season with salt, if desired. You can run some or all of the sauce through a food processor or use an immersion blender.

ANGRY PENNE:
In a large pot on high heat, bring 6 qt/L water to a boil. Add penne and salt and cook to desired tenderness. Drain and toss with hot Arrabiata Sauce. Sprinkle each serving with parsley.

Roasted Cauliflower

This dish is a chameleon, as comfortable when paired with Indian flavors as with Mediterranean. Unfussy and appetizing.

1 cauliflower head	1 tsp ground cumin
½ tsp kosher salt	1 tsp cumin seeds
½ tsp ground coriander	4 tbsp olive oil

Seed savers: Whole coriander and cumin seeds take on a rich smokiness when toasted before cooking. Lightly toast whole spices in a non-stick frying pan until fragrant before grinding.

Preheat oven to 425°F (220°C).

Cut cauliflower into about 12 pieces and place in a large mixing bowl. Sprinkle with salt, coriander, cumin, and cumin seeds. Drizzle with olive oil and toss to coat.

Place in a large ceramic baking dish and bake for 40 minutes, until edges are brown and cauliflower is fork tender.

Green Beans with Pepitas

This is a great way to jazz up green beans and a perfect side to grilled meats.

1 tbsp olive oil

½ cup (125 mL) pepitas (shelled pumpkin seeds)

1 garlic clove, thinly sliced

1 tbsp chopped fresh rosemary

½ tsp kosher salt

1 lb (500 g) green beans, trimmed

In a non-stick frying pan on medium, heat olive oil. Sauté pepitas for 2 minutes. Add garlic, rosemary, and salt and sauté until fragrant.

In a large pot of boiling water, blanch green beans until tender but firm, about 2 minutes. Drain and toss with pepita mixture.

Grilled Autumn Vegetables

Grilling enhances the sweetness of vegetables by caramelizing natural sugars and making them taste more intensely like themselves.

MAKES 4–6 SERVINGS

2 tbsp olive oil

½ tsp sea salt

¼ tsp ground black pepper

zest of 1 lemon

1 tbsp lemon juice

8 baby carrots, halved lengthwise

1 cup (250 mL) green beans, trimmed

1 small zucchini, halved and quartered

2 tbsp chopped fresh chives or dill

In a large, flat dish, combine olive oil, salt, pepper, and lemon zest and juice to make a marinade.

In a large pot of boiling water, blanch carrots for 3 minutes and set aside. Blanch green beans for 1 minute and set aside. Toss carrots, beans, and zucchini in marinade and set aside for 30 minutes.

Preheat barbecue to high. Position vegetables across the grill so that they don't fall through. Grill until grill-marks and caramelizing are evident, about 2–3 minutes. Serve sprinkled with chopped chives or dill.

Bacon & Mushroom Kale

This is a quick way to brighten up humble leafy greens. To remove the stalk from the kale, grab the bottom of the stalk with your left hand and run the thumb and forefinger of your right hand where the leaf is attached firmly up the stalk from the bottom.

MAKES 4–6 SERVINGS

1 tbsp olive oil

3 slices bacon, chopped

12 fresh cremini mushrooms, sliced

12 kale leaves (4 cups/1 L chopped)

¼ tsp kosher salt

¼ cup (60 mL) low-sodium chicken or
   vegetable stock

In a large saucepan on medium, heat olive oil. Add bacon and sauté until crisp. Remove bacon from pan and set aside. Add mushrooms. Don't stir until they begin to brown, about 2 minutes.

Stir in kale leaves, salt, and stock, turning leaves over to wilt. Simmer for 5 minutes. Top with bacon.

Duck Fat Rosemary Potatoes

This is a great way to use early potatoes (before they get too big) or undersized spuds at the end of season. This recipe includes an old trick to create a rough, crunchy crust, which my youngest son declared the "best thing ever."

MAKES 4 SERVINGS

2 lb (1 kg) Yukon Gold potatoes, peeled and cut in large chunks

1½ tbsp kosher salt

¼ cup (60 mL) duck fat (or canola oil)

6-in (15-cm) sprig fresh rosemary

¼ tsp fine sea salt

¼ tsp fresh ground black pepper

2 tbsp chopped fresh rosemary leaves

Look for duck fat at gourmet food stores, good butcher shops, and high-end grocers. There is no substitute.

Don't panic at the amount of salt in the water; it has to season a lot of potatoes, and most of it will go down the drain later.

Preheat oven to 425°F (220°C).

In a medium saucepan on high heat, bring potatoes, 3 cups (750 mL) water, and salt to a boil. Simmer until fork tender on outside but firm inside, about 5–10 minutes depending on the size of your potatoes. Drain potatoes, cover with a lid and place pan on cold stove burner or other flat, unheated surface. Hold lid and handle firmly and shake pot vigorously for 5 seconds, until outsides of potatoes look rough and fluffy. Set potatoes aside, uncovered.

Place a metal roasting pan in oven for 5 minutes to preheat. Add duck fat and let it warm for 5 minutes. Using tongs, swish rosemary sprig through oil, then add potatoes, turning to coat them with fat. Bake for 25 minutes. Turn potatoes for even browning, then roast for another 20 minutes, until golden brown and crunchy. Sprinkle with salt and pepper. Transfer to a serving dish and garnish with rosemary leaves.

Roasted Garlic Mashed Potatoes

Warm, rustic, and deeply flavorful, these mashed potatoes are reason enough to grow garlic. Serve garnished with Parmesan Fricos (p. 165).

MAKES 4 SERVINGS

6 cups (1.5 L) diced Yukon Gold potatoes	¼ cup (60 mL) unsalted butter
2 tsp kosher salt, divided	½ cup (125 mL) cream
¼ tsp white pepper	2 roasted garlic bulbs (p. 141)

In a saucepan on high heat, bring potatoes and 1 tsp salt to a boil in 2 cups (500 mL) cold water. Reduce heat and cook at a high simmer until knife tender, about 5–7 minutes. Drain and return potatoes to pot.

Add pepper, butter, cream, and remainder of salt. Squeeze garlic bulbs to press out flesh and add to potatoes. Mash potatoes just until smooth.

Cheddar Dill Biscuits

My late father Frank Shore was as traditional a high school teacher as you'd ever meet, but in some ways a little ahead of his time. At a moment in history when hardly anyone considered teaching boys to cook, he developed a course called Bachelor Survival and encouraged a steady stream of boys—many of them covered in wood chips and engine grime—to exit the shop building and learn to cook. This is my riff on one of his core lessons, and it includes my labor-saving trick of freezing then grating the butter. Fluffy inside and crunchy outside, this biscuit is a delicious vehicle for butter, cheese, or gravy.

MAKES 8 BISCUITS

¼ cup (60 mL) unsalted butter

2 cups (500 mL) all-purpose flour

2½ tsp baking powder

½ tsp baking soda

½ tsp kosher salt

½ cup (125 mL) grated cheddar cheese

¼ cup (60 mL) chopped fresh dill fronds

¾ cup + 1 tbsp (200 mL) buttermilk

1 egg, beaten

Place butter and grater in freezer for 1 hour.

Preheat oven to 450°F (230°C).

In a bowl, whisk flour, baking powder and soda, salt, cheese, and dill. Remove butter from freezer and coarsely grate over flour mixture. Add buttermilk and stir in gently with a fork until a dough forms. Knead dough gently with your hands until it just forms a ball, no more than 30 seconds.

Sprinkle flour on work surface and turn out dough. Roll to ¾-in (2-cm) thickness in as few strokes as possible. Cut into 3-in (8-cm) rounds with a water glass or cookie cutter. Re-form remaining dough, roll, and cut 1 or 2 more rounds.

Place rounds on a cookie sheet and let stand for 10 minutes.

In a small bowl, whisk egg and brush over tops of biscuits. Place cookie sheet on middle rack of oven and bake for 13 minutes, until golden brown, slightly shiny, and springy to the touch.

Frank Shore's Dumplings

Here's a classic from the pages of my father's arsenal of farmhouse recipes. These fluffy delights are meant to steam on top of a hearty stew such Chicken Fricassee (p. 39). Use whatever garden herbs are in abundance.

(p. 39)

MAKES ENOUGH FOR 4 SERVINGS (12 DUMPLINGS)

1 cup (250 mL) all-purpose flour

2 tsp baking powder

½ tsp kosher salt

1 tbsp chopped fresh parsley

1 tbsp chopped fresh chives

1 egg

about ⅓ cup (80 mL) milk

Don't submerge or boil the dumplings.

While stew, fricassee, or soup is simmering in a large, wide-based pot: In a large bowl, whisk flour, baking powder, and salt. Stir in parsley and chives. Break egg into a measuring cup and top up to ½ cup (125 mL) line with milk.

Whisk wet ingredients to combine well and stir into dry ingredients and herbs. The result should be thicker than a batter, but looser than dough. Add a little milk if dough doesn't ooze.

Using a tablespoon, quickly drop a dozen dumplings on top of simmering stew. Leave 1 in (2.5 cm) between dumplings so they can expand. Cover pot with a tight-fitting lid and steam dumplings for 10 minutes. Serve immediately.

Parmesan Fricos

A Parmesan frico is possibly the best tasting thing you will ever eat. Think aged-cheese cookie. Stand one of these crispy delights in the mashed potatoes when you build plates for dinner guests. Result: You are a genius.

MAKES 6 SERVINGS

1 cup (250 mL) finely grated Parmesan cheese

¼ tsp ground black pepper

Preheat oven to 500°F (260°C).

Place a sheet of parchment paper on a cookie sheet. Place 2 tbsp cheese in a cookie-sized circle about ¼-in (6-mm) thick. Leave it fluffy, not pressed down. Sprinkle lightly with pepper.

Bake for 4–6 minutes until they turn a golden brown at edges. Do not take your eyes off them until they are done: they'll go from golden to incinerated in a heartbeat. Cool on cookie sheet for 5 minutes.

Apple-Pear Streusel

The perfect autumn dessert, this streusel-topped confection is actually easier than pie.

MAKES 4–6 SERVINGS

FILLING:

2 lb (1 kg) Bosc pears

2 lb (1 kg) green apples

2 tsp grated orange zest

2 tbsp orange juice

1 tbsp lemon juice

½ cup (125 mL) white sugar

2 tbsp cornstarch

1 tsp ground cinnamon

¼ tsp ground nutmeg

TOPPING:

1½ cups (375 mL) flour

¾ cup (185 mL) white sugar

¾ cup (185 mL) brown sugar

1 cup (250 mL) rolled oats

1 cup (250 mL) salted butter

Preheat oven to 350°F (180°C).

Peel, core, and cut pears and apples into ¼-in (6-mm) thick slices. In a large bowl, combine pears, apples, zest, orange and lemon juice, sugar, cornstarch, cinnamon, and nutmeg. Pour into a 9 x 12-in (23 x 30.5-cm) baking dish.

In bowl of a stand mixer fitted with a paddle attachment, combine flour, white and brown sugar, oats, and butter. Mix on low for 1 minute, until mixture forms large clumps. Sprinkle evenly over fruit. Bake for 1 hour, until top is browned and filling bubbling.

Winter

Enjoy the Bounty

When the rain and snow finally force me indoors for the winter, I take the extra time to reflect on the growing season—its successes and failures. The years of experimentation have taught me some harsh lessons, but each lesson learned has rewarded me with greater abundance and increased my family's self-reliance.

Two freezers loaded with the garden's harvest—whole tomatoes, chopped rhubarb, grated zucchini, blanched green beans—help take the sting out of the weekly grocery bill. When the produce at the market begins to look shabby due to harsh winter weather and days spent in transit from warmer climes, a pantry full of crimson pickled beets and bright green dills is reassuring. Vegetables that are picked and preserved at the peak of ripeness retain more of their nutritional value than so-called fresh produce that's spent days in the back of a truck.

Food industry experts and economic think-tanks insist that long-distance travel contributes only a tiny fraction to the carbon footprint of fruits and vegetables grown abroad, especially when foreign farmers can grow more efficiently. Maybe so. But the vitamin and antioxidant content of freshly picked vegetables begins to decline within hours and drops by forty to ninety percent over three days. Food grown closer to home is likely to be much fresher and better for you. If it isn't in your garden, check the local farmer's market.

A CASE FOR THE BACKYARD GREENHOUSE

I decided to buy a greenhouse whether the economics made sense or not. Something about a tax return check makes me irrational. No apparatus will extend the growing season more reliably than a greenhouse, and five years into my experiment, I am now in a position to justify the expense.

A greenhouse kit, complete with double-glazed walls, a door, and vents will cost you anywhere from $600 to $6,000, depending on quality of build, size, and whether you opt for polycarbonate or glass walls. I spent about $2,000 for a poly-walled structure with 64 sq. ft (5.9 sq. m) of interior space and a heat-responsive vent. I invested another $200 in pre-cast concrete tiles for the floor.

So what did I gain? I grow lettuce and parsley right through the winter, adding at least four months to the growing season. I grow most of my own seedlings for transplanting to the garden

in spring. I grow cherry tomatoes, hot peppers, and basil through the summer. I seed pots with leftover kale, beet, and arugula seeds in the fall and harvest baby greens until Christmas.

The annual value of produce from my greenhouse is at least $500 a year. The basil alone is worth $200 when you consider the price of pesto at the grocery store. My wife and I make huge batches of Basil Pesto (p. 76) in August and freeze twenty to thirty small containers to use through the cooler months.

Organic seedlings can cost three to five dollars each at the nursery, but growing them at home costs no more than twenty-five cents, including the cost of potting soil. Cherry tomatoes can cost six dollars for a small basket at the grocery store, but I can pick two to three pints a week from the greenhouse during the summer. See how it adds up?

GROW SPROUTS ON YOUR KITCHEN COUNTER

You don't need a garden or even a balcony to grow crisp fresh bean and alfalfa sprouts. A 1 qt/L Mason jar, a sealing ring, and a small square of cheesecloth is all the equipment you need. You won't even get your hands dirty—no soil required.

Buy organic beans and alfalfa seeds for sprouting at a health food store. Radish seed and lentils added to the mix make for an interesting sprout blend for salads. At room temperature, the usual sprouting time is about four to six days. Once the seeds sprout and grow to the appropriate size, rinse them and keep refrigerated.

Start a new jar of sprouts every weekend for a supply of sprouts right through the winter.

1. Measure ¼ cup (60 mL) beans or seed mix into jar.

2. Cut a piece of cheesecloth about 6 sq. in (38 sq. cm) and cover the jar opening. Screw a sealing ring over cheesecloth to hold it in place.

3. Fill jar with fresh, cold water and let stand for twelve hours.

4. Drain and refill jar with water to rinse seeds and beans. Drain and lay jar on its side, out of direct sunlight. Cover with a tea towel to block light.

5. Refill jar with cold fresh water and drain every twelve hours. Keep jar covered between rinses.

Makes 2–4 cups (500 mL–1 L) sprouts.

Place sprouted alfalfa in a bright location for one day to turn the leaves green, then refrigerate until needed.

HABITS OF HEALTHY PEOPLE

Be wary of any headline that promises a magic bullet solution to increased vigor, weight loss, or longer life. Even properly designed studies that suggest fish oil can prevent heart attacks should be viewed with caution. When you look closely at the evidence, you'll find that eating fish helps; fish oil supplements do not.

Science looks at biological processes such as energy metabolism through a tiny keyhole, isolating each moving part in a large and very complex machine. Scientists also tend to study these processes in animal models, which helps to isolate specific effects in mice. The results usually have little to do with how human beings live their lives.

Promoters of diet products seize on these results and manipulate and distort them to sell supplements of dubious value. Most of the well-known diet supplements are simply fruit extracts or inexpensive dietary fiber packaged in capsules and sold for 100 times their wholesale price.

The scientific truth about long life and better health is decidedly mundane. Vitamins and supplements in capsules or pills confer little or no benefit to healthy people. Dozens of studies involving tens of thousands of people confirm that simple fact. If scientists using razor-sharp statistical tools and carefully controlled experiments can't detect any health effects in people who consume these products, it probably isn't there. Supplements can be useful to treat a deficiency identified by your doctor, but they're not much help otherwise.

However, a handful of communities scattered across the globe may provide some clues in the search for a longer, healthier life. The world is home to five small groups of people who live far longer than the rest of us. People in these so-called Blue Zones are far more likely to live into their nineties and some have ten times the usual proportion of centenarians. So, what makes the lifestyle special in mountainous Sardinia, isolated Japanese and Greek islands, Costa Rican villages, and Loma Linda, California?

Blue Zones have three things in common. All are small, relatively isolated, family-oriented, and socially tight-knit. The people are active, walking almost everywhere, and grow at least some of their own food. And with the exception of Sardinia, they eat a mostly plant-based diet, rich in leafy greens and legumes, such as lentils and beans. Sardinians who cover a lot of steep terrain on foot each day appear to extend their lives by years.

In fact, science tends to support the value of social engagement, daily physical activity, and a diet rich in fiber, fruit, vegetables, nuts, and healthy fats. The key to longer life is probably right outside your window—in the garden or a short walk away at your local farmer's market.

EAT PLANT-BASED MEALS AND LIKE IT

If vegetarian meals leave you feeling a little bit empty inside, you are not alone. Like many people, I have dabbled in vegetarianism, originally out of poverty and later for my health. Some people eliminate meat from their diets because they feel that it's unethical to kill animals for food. But for me, the most compelling reason to eat less meat is the environmental impact of commercial meat production. The amount of arable land required to produce one lb (500 g) of animal protein is roughly five times that needed to grow corn. Soy beans are twenty times more efficient than cattle at creating quality protein for human consumption. The quantity of water required to produce beef may be up to 100 times the amount required to produce grain such as wheat.

As the world's population continues to grow, the amount of fertilizer that can be used to increase food production is reaching its upper limit. Land and water are finite resources. You don't have to be a rocket scientist to understand that we must inevitably turn to a more plant-based diet. Human beings and livestock are becoming increasingly incompatible. The price of meat in the future will surely reflect this, curtailing consumption. In the meantime, you can help preserve the earth's limited resources by adopting a diet with a lighter footprint.

Meat substitutes are a double-edged sword: On one hand, commercially made vegetarian cutlets, skewers, and patties deliver the protein you are accustomed to and provide meat-like texture. But they are often high in sodium and use a lot of processed ingredients. I think foods should be what they are and not pretend to be what they are not. But the market for soy-based meat substitutes has quadrupled in the past fifteen years, so they must be appealing to a lot of people.

By far the most common complaint I hear from people, especially men, who attempt semi-vegetarian eating is persistent hunger. If you want to reduce your meat consumption, you don't have to starve yourself. Start with one meatless meal a week, and work your way up until you find your comfort zone. Fruit and oatmeal for breakfast is an easy way to start. Leaving meat out of the lunch I bring to the office works well for me, too. At dinner, I simply cut back on the amount of meat on my plate and make sure that I have a good high-protein dish based on chickpeas, lentils, or beans to pick up the slack.

Here are a few tips to help you enjoy more plant-based meals.

Don't forget protein: Meatless Monday is doomed to fail if you don't feel full after dinner. Simply removing meat from your stir-fry is a recipe for disaster. Try replacing chicken with cashews. Adding nuts and seeds, whole grains, and legumes at mealtime promotes long-lasting fullness.

Eat fat: A dinner without meat often results in an overall reduction in fats. But good fats are an essential nutrient that promotes satiety. If you avoid fat and also reduce the meat protein in your meals, you may soon find yourself sitting in front of a double cheeseburger with no recollection of having bought it. Oily fish, walnuts and cashews, and quality cooking fats such as olive oil will keep your stomach from rumbling, and they will also ensure that you get sufficient quantities of heart-healthy omega-3 fatty acids and fat-soluble vitamins.

Adopt an ethnic cuisine: If your plan is to go without meat one day a week, plan an Asian meal. Many of the world's oldest food traditions are based on non-meat proteins such as soy and legumes. Dishes from India and Turkey rely heavily on lentils, beans, and chickpeas. Plan a meal around Red Lentil Dal (p. 58), Chickpea Salad with Cilantro Pesto (p. 34) or Malai Kofta (p. 96).

Whole grains are your friend: Whole grains are higher in fiber and protein than refined grains and flours. They will keep you full longer than simple carbohydrates such as potatoes and white flour pasta. Bulgur is the cracked durum wheat at the heart of Herbed Tabbouleh (p. 35). Kamut is a whole berry that's an ancient relative of wheat. Try it in Pharoah Salad (p. 84).

EAT LESS BUT BETTER MEAT

When you do buy meat, you can help yourself and the planet by choosing pasture-raised chicken and grass-fed beef. Most organic certifications

require farmers to ensure that their animals are humanely treated and fed a natural diet. Not only is that the moral thing to do, it's better for you too.

Grass-fed beef has a more favorable ratio (for human health) of omega-3 to omega-6 fatty acids than factory-farmed beef. Recent research has found that excessive omega-6 consumption may be associated with inflammation of the cardiovascular system and the digestive tract. Pasture-raised chicken tends to be lower in fat overall and, like grass-fed beef, much higher in heart-healthy omega-3.

Get to know a good butcher and ask for grass-fed meats. A farmer's market is a great place to source pasture-raised meats and, as a bonus, the farmer is right there to answer your questions about how the animal was raised and what it was fed.

Roasted Red Pepper Hummus

Hummus, the creamy dip beloved in the Middle East, is easily made in a food processor with chickpeas, tahini, olive oil, and a squeeze of lemon. Unglamorous and under-appreciated, the chickpea is an inexpensive, earth-friendly source of protein and carbohydrates and an extraordinary source of dietary fiber. If you like to dig deep when you dip—like I do—dig into this hummus without guilt. Serve with Super Simple Pita Bread (p. 62), crackers, chips, and veggies.

MAKES 2 CUPS (500 ML)

2 cups (500 mL) cooked chickpeas, or 1 19-oz (540-mL) can, drained and rinsed

2 tbsp tahini

2 garlic cloves

1 roasted red pepper (p. 45)

1 tsp coarse sea salt

3 tbsp lemon juice

¼ cup (60 mL) extra virgin olive oil

Kalamata olives, for garnish

extra virgin olive oil, for garnish

In a food processor, blend chickpeas, tahini, garlic, pepper, salt, lemon juice, and olive oil until smooth. Pour into a bowl, garnish with olives, and drizzle lightly with more olive oil.

Herbed Ricotta Spread

Dreamy, creamy goodness. This is why bread was invented.
Serve it on a thinly sliced toasted baguette.

MAKES I CUP (250 ML)

1 cup (250 mL) Homemade Ricotta Cheese
   (p. 199)

¼ cup (60 mL) chopped fresh chives

1 tsp kosher salt

½ tsp ground black pepper

2 tsp lemon zest

2 tbsp lemon juice

2 tbsp unfiltered olive oil, divided

chopped fresh chives, for garnish

In a bowl, combine cheese, chives, salt, pepper, lemon zest and juice, and 1 tbsp olive oil. Mix with a fork until creamy. Let stand for 1 hour. Transfer to serving dish, drizzle with remainder of olive oil, and garnish with chopped chives.

Homemade Chicken Stock

Rich, homemade stock can elevate ordinary home cooking to extraordinary cooking. Stock can make simple rice into an epiphany. It also makes homemade soup a breeze. If you need more reasons to make homemade stock, how about weight management, healthy joints and bones, and smooth skin? Drink a bowl of broth before lunch and supper and you will eat less and stay full longer. Homemade stock contains quality amino acids, calcium, phosphorus, magnesium, silicon, and all kinds of other trace minerals and vitamins. Why not extract every bit of goodness from your food before you throw it away? That's sustainable living, baby.

MAKES ABOUT 8 CUPS (2 L) (YIELD MAY VARY)

3 lb (1.5 kg) chicken backs, wing tips, and bones

1 onion, quartered

2 carrots

1 tbsp canola oil

1 tsp kosher salt

¼ tsp ground black pepper

Preheat oven to 400°F (200°C).

Place chicken, onions, and carrots on a large baking sheet with a minimum ½-in (1-cm) rim. Drizzle with oil and sprinkle with salt and pepper. Bake until chicken is golden and fat is rendered out, about 1 hour.

In a large stock pot on medium-low heat, add chicken, onions, and carrots (and any other leftover vegetable trimmings). Add cold water until covered. Pour 2 cups (500 mL) boiling water on baking sheet and let sit for 2 minutes. Use a wooden spoon to loosen baked-on chicken juices and pour resulting slurry into stock pot.

Slowly bring temperature of cooking liquid to 190°F (87°C). Do not let it boil. Cook uncovered for 3 hours. Skim fat off with a ladle or gravy separator. Pour liquid through a colander lined with cheesecloth and discard bones and vegetables. Store stock in refrigerator for up to 1 week or freeze in plastic containers and thaw as needed.

Chicken Stock

TIPS FOR EASY STOCK MAKING
Save vegetable trimmings.
When you cook, keep the
carrot ends, celery base, onion
ends and skin, and parsley
stems in a bowl on the counter
and store in the refrigerator
(or in a ziplock bag in the
freezer) until stock day. Heck,
it's actually easier than throwing them away.

*Cut the back out of every
chicken you cook.* Take off the
wing tips too—nobody eats
them anyway. I keep a large
zip-lock bag in the freezer to
store chicken backs and wings.

When you have six to ten
chicken backs in the freezer,
it's stock day.

**THINGS TO DO WITH HOMEMADE
STOCK**
Make vegetable soup: Simmer
diced vegetables in stock and
add a handful of small pasta,
rice, or barley. Kale Chickpea
Soup (p. 178) is both nutritious
and delicious.

Make better gravy: Stock adds
body and flavor to gravy and
sauces without adding fat.

*Make Randy's favorite
breakfast*: Garden-Style Wor
Wonton Soup (p. 32). Add
a few broccoli florets, some
homemade wontons (p. 33),
and some shredded Napa
cabbage to chicken stock
and you'll have a serving of
vegetables in you before you
even leave the house.

Drink broth before dinner:
Broth is nutritious and fat-
free. Add a few blocks of tofu,
miso paste, and chopped green
onions. Did I mention that
you will eat less and stay full
longer?

Kale Chickpea Soup

This soup is so simple it's hardly even a recipe. But we eat it at least weekly as a light lunch. It's high in fiber and antioxidants, soul-satisfying, and tummy warming. Use canned or cooked frozen chickpeas to save time. If you have a tub of stock lying around in the freezer, thaw it out. If you made a bit of stock from the bones of last night's chicken dinner, use that. If not, use low-sodium chicken stock from the grocery store.

MAKES 4 SERVINGS

5 cups (1.25 L) Homemade (p. 176) or low-sodium chicken stock

¾ cup (160 mL) dried macaroni

1 cup (250 mL) chopped lacinato kale

1 cup (250 mL) cooked chickpeas

sea salt, to taste

¼ cup (60 mL) chopped green onions

1 tbsp chopped fresh parsley

When cooking with stock of unknown sodium content, hold back on adding salt until the cooking liquid has had time to interact with the other ingredients. Taste your dish before adding salt to any recipe that includes stock.

In a large saucepan on medium-high heat, bring stock to a boil. Add macaroni, boil for 2 minutes, reduce heat to low, and simmer for 5 minutes. Add kale and simmer for another 5 minutes. Add chickpeas and simmer until heated through.

Taste and season with salt to taste, if desired. Serve in bowls garnished with green onions and parsley. That's it. You're done.

Matzoh Ball Soup

This is Jewish penicillin, the only known cure for the Man Cold.
My wife Darcy makes it when cold season arrives. It may not be backed
by science, but I'd swear that this soup can cure a virus.

MAKES 4 SERVINGS

MATZOH BALLS:

½ cup (125 mL) matzoh meal

2 tbsp chopped fresh chives

2 tbsp chopped fresh parsley

¼ tsp kosher salt

⅛ tsp ground black pepper

2 eggs, lightly beaten

2 tbsp *schmaltz* (rendered chicken fat) or melted butter

SOUP:

2 tbsp *schmaltz* or butter

½ cup (125 mL) chopped green onions

½ cup (125 mL) diced onions

½ cup (125 mL) diced carrots

½ cup (125 mL) diced celery

¼ cup (60 mL) dry white wine

6 cups (1.5 L) Homemade or low-sodium chicken stock (p. 176)

sea salt, to taste

2 tbsp chopped fresh parsley

2 tbsp chopped fresh chives

In a bowl, mix matzoh meal, chives, parsley, salt, and pepper. Add eggs and 2 tbsp *schmaltz* to dry ingredients and mix until combined, then begin to add 3–4 tbsp water, 1 tbsp at a time, just until a thick batter forms. Refrigerate batter for 30 minutes.

Meanwhile, in a large saucepan on medium, heat 2 tbsp *schmaltz*. Add green onions, onions, carrots, and celery and sauté until soft, about 5 minutes. Add wine and cook until reduced by half, about 3 minutes. Add stock and simmer for 15 minutes. Season to taste with salt, if desired

In a large pot on high, bring 2 qt/L water to a simmer. Add 1 tbsp kosher salt. Use a spoon to shape matzoh dough into balls and drop into stock. Simmer for 30 minutes. Add matzoh balls to hot soup and serve. Garnish with parsley and chives.

Canadian Caldo Verde

There are as many recipes for this hearty Portuguese soup as there are kitchens in Portugal. This Canadian version uses Yukon Gold potatoes and lacinato kale.

MAKES 6 SERVINGS

2 tbsp extra virgin olive oil

1½ cups (375 mL) diced onions

5 oz (150 g) cured chorizo sausages, diced

1 tsp sweet smoked paprika

½ tsp hot smoked paprika

4 cups (1 L) sliced Yukon Gold potatoes

4 cups (1 L) Homemade (p. 176) or low-sodium chicken stock

1½ tsp kosher salt, or to taste

2 packed cups (500 mL) chopped lacinato kale

In a large pot on medium, heat olive oil. Add onions and chorizo and cook until onions are soft and fat begins to render from chorizo, about 10 minutes. Add sweet and hot paprika and stir for about 1 minute, then add potatoes and stir to coat. Add stock and bring to a boil, then reduce heat and simmer with lid on for 5 minutes. Taste and season with salt. Add kale and simmer for 20 minutes. Use a potato masher to break up potatoes, just until soup thickens to your liking.

Pea Soup with Carrots

Carrots add sweetness and freshness to this split pea soup. Find the biggest smoked ham hock you can; the really meaty ones not only add a lot flavor, but you can pick the meat off the bones later and add it to the soup.

1 ham hock

3 tbsp olive oil

1 cup (250 mL) diced onions

1 cup (250 mL) diced celery

2 cups (500 mL) diced carrots

1 tsp kosher salt

½ tsp ground black pepper

1 tsp fresh thyme leaves

1 lb (500 g) dried split peas

2 fresh bay leaves

In a large pot on high heat, cover ham hock with 10 cups (2.4 L) water. Bring to a boil, then reduce heat and simmer for 1 hour. Remove ham hock and set aside to cool. Reserve cooking liquid.

In a separate pot on medium, heat olive oil. Sauté onions, celery, carrots, salt, pepper, and thyme leaves until vegetables are tender, about 7 minutes. Add 8 cups (2 L) cooking liquid, split peas, and bay leaves. Increase heat to high and bring to a boil for 1 minute. Reduce heat to low and simmer for 2 hours. Add more cooking liquid, if necessary.

Shred meat from ham hock, discarding skin, fat and bones, add meat to soup pot, and heat through.

Beer-Battered Fish

If you want to blow some minds, serve this crispy beer-battered fish on top of Singapore Curry Sauce (p. 207). It's weird, but it works. Search the Ocean Wise website for sustainable fish suggestions.

MAKES 4 SERVINGS

2-3 cups (500-750 mL) canola oil, for frying

1 lb (500 g) Pacific cod or other white fish

1 tsp kosher salt, divided

1 cup (250 mL) flour

1 tsp baking powder

1 tsp sweet paprika

¾ cup (185 mL) cold pale ale

Preheat oil in a deep pot to 350°F (180°C).

Cut the fish into strips 1–1½ in (2.5–4 cm) wide and 3 in (8 cm) long. Season fish with ½ tsp salt. In a large bowl, whisk flour, baking powder, paprika, and remainder of salt with pale ale.

Place fish in batter and coat completely. Pick up fish pieces and let excess batter run off. Gently place fish in hot oil and deep fry for 3–4 minutes, until golden brown. Be careful when working with hot oil! Cook in batches to avoid crowding the pan. Drain on paper towels.

Smoked Salmon Chowder

Rich, creamy, and smoky, this soup is perfect for a crisp winter day.

MAKES 4 SERVINGS

2 tbsp butter

½ cup (125 mL) minced leeks

½ cup (125 mL) diced celery

1 tsp celery salt

4 cups (1 L) salmon (see sidebar) or
   vegetable stock

4 cups (1 L) diced potatoes

½ cup (125 mL) all-purpose flour

1 cup (250 mL) cream

6–12 oz (175–340 g) hot smoked salmon,
   crumbled

¼ tsp white pepper

sea salt, to taste

¼ cup (60 mL) chopped chives

Simple Salmon Stock: Simmer head, tail, and bones of 1 sockeye salmon and 1 quartered onion in 5 cups (1.25 L) water and ½ tsp kosher salt for 1 hour. Strain through a colander lined with two layers of cheesecloth.

In a large pot on medium heat, melt butter. Add leeks, celery, and celery salt. Sauté until vegetables soften, about 4 minutes. Increase heat to high, add stock and potatoes, and bring to a boil for 1 minute. Reduce heat to medium-low and simmer until potatoes soften, about 10 minutes.

In a bowl, whisk flour and cream, then slowly add mixture to pot while stirring. You may not use all of cream mixture; don't over-thicken chowder. Add salmon and pepper and simmer gently for 5 minutes. Season to taste with salt. To serve, top bowls of chowder with chives.

Chicken & Sausage Gumbo

This gumbo is thickened with a traditional dark roux and filé, a.k.a. gumbo powder, made of ground sassafras leaves. We use leftover chicken as the main protein, but rabbit and pork also work well. Serve gumbo as a hearty soup or as a meal with rice.

MAKES 4–8 SERVINGS

- ¼ cup (60 mL) olive oil
- ¼ cup (60 mL) vegetable oil
- ½ lb (250 g) andouille sausage, diced
- ¾ cup (180 mL) all-purpose flour
- 2 cups (500 mL) diced onions
- 1 cup (250 mL) diced celery
- 2 bell peppers, chopped
- 4 garlic cloves, minced
- 4 cups (1 L) low-sodium chicken stock

- ¼ tsp chipotle powder
- ¼ tsp ground black pepper
- 2 tsp smoked paprika
- 1 tsp fresh thyme leaves
- 1 tsp fresh oregano leaves
- 1 tsp filé powder (optional)
- 1–2 tsp kosher salt
- 1 lb (500 g) shredded cooked chicken
- ½ cup (125 mL) chopped green onions

In a large flat-bottomed pan on medium, heat oils. Fry sausages until browned, about 5 minutes. Remove sausages with a slotted spoon and set aside. Whisk in flour and cook on medium-low heat, stirring frequently, until roux is brown, about the color of a brick. Don't let it burn.

Add onions, celery, and bell peppers, and stir into roux to cook until softened, about 3 minutes. Add garlic and stock, stirring until mixture thickens. Add chipotle, pepper, paprika, thyme, oregano, filé, and 1 tsp salt and simmer for 30 minutes.

Add sausages and shredded chicken and simmer for another 30–60 minutes. Taste and season with remainder of salt, if desired. Stir in green onions.

Chicken alla Cacciatore

This is a vegetable-forward version of the classic Italian hunter's meal.
If you froze large numbers of tomatoes last summer, this is your opportunity
to use some of them. Simmer 2 lb (1 kg) frozen tomatoes for 15 minutes
and substitute them for fresh tomatoes.

MAKES 4–6 SERVINGS

3–4 lb (1.4–1.8 kg) chicken, cut into pieces

2 tsp kosher salt, divided

½ tsp ground black pepper

2 tbsp extra virgin olive oil

2 cups (500 mL) diced onions

1 green bell pepper, diced

1 carrot, minced

2 celery stalks, minced

1 garlic clove, minced

10 plum tomatoes, diced

1 5.5-oz (160-g) tin tomato paste

¼ cup (60 mL) white wine

3 tbsp fresh oregano leaves

2 tbsp kosher salt, for pasta water

1 lb (500 g) dried penne

¼ cup (60 mL) chopped fresh parsley

Preheat oven to 325°F (160°C).

Season chicken with 1 tsp salt and pepper. In a large, oven-proof pot on medium, heat olive oil. Add chicken pieces 4 at a time (do not overcrowd pot). Cook on each side until brown, about 8 minutes in total. Remove chicken from pot and set aside. Sauté onions, bell peppers, carrots, celery, and garlic in pot until soft, about 5 minutes. Stir in 1 tsp salt, tomatoes, tomato paste, and wine, and simmer for 5 minutes. Add oregano. Return chicken to pot and immerse in sauce. Bring to a boil, and then cover pot and bake for 1 hour. Remove chicken and set aside.

In a separate pot on high heat, boil 6 qt/L water. Stir in 2 tbsp salt and penne. Cook at a low boil for 6 minutes. Drain pasta and add to sauce mixture. Stir to combine, then simmer on low heat for 5 minutes. Transfer pasta and sauce to a large serving dish, top with chicken pieces, and sprinkle with parsley.

Turkey Meatballs

Light and bright with herb flavors and subtle spices, turkey meatballs make a great appetizer on their own or a tasty protein boost for Singapore Curry Sauce with Kale (p. 207) or in Stuffed Spaghetti Squash (p. 188).

MAKES ABOUT 16 MEATBALLS

1 lb (500 g) ground turkey

3 tbsp plain bread crumbs

1 egg

1 tsp kosher salt

½ tsp ground cumin

¼ tsp ground coriander

½ tsp ground black pepper

2 tbsp canola oil, for frying

In a bowl, combine turkey, bread crumbs, egg, salt, cumin, coriander, and pepper, and mix with your hands for about 30 seconds. Roll 1½ tbsp of mixture between your palms to form meatballs.

In a frying pan on medium, heat canola oil. Fry meatballs until evenly browned and firm to the touch, about 5 minutes.

Stuffed Spaghetti Squash

Make spaghetti squash the foundation of a tasty, light meal.
You can substitute chopped ham for the meatballs, or leave the meat
out altogether for a vegetarian meal.

MAKES 2–4 SERVINGS

1 medium-sized spaghetti squash

2 tbsp olive oil

¾ cup (185 mL) diced onions

¾ cup (185 mL) diced celery

½ cup (125 mL) sliced mushrooms

1 carrot, minced

1 garlic clove, minced

½ tsp kosher salt

4 Italian Sausage Meatballs (p. 50), cooked
and roughly chopped

1 cup (250 mL) fresh baby spinach

¼ cup (60 mL) bread crumbs

¼ cup (60 mL) grated provolone cheese

¾ cup (185 mL) Spicy Arrabiata Sauce
(p. 156)

¼ tsp dried marjoram

¼ tsp dried basil

¼ tsp dried thyme leaves

¼ tsp ground black pepper

½ cup (250 mL) grated mozzarella cheese

¼ cup (60 mL) grated Edam cheese

2 tbsp grated Parmesan cheese

Preheat oven to 375°F (190°C).

Halve squash lengthwise and scrape out seeds. In a large pot on high heat, bring 4 qt/L water to a boil and cook squash for 10 minutes.

Remove and set aside to cool.

In a large sauté pan on medium, heat olive oil. Sauté onions, celery, mushrooms, carrots, garlic, and salt until vegetables are softened, about 5 minutes.

With a large spoon, remove flesh from squash and place in a large bowl. Add vegetable mixture, meatballs, spinach, bread crumbs, provolone, Arrabiata Sauce, marjoram, basil, thyme, and pepper. Mix to combine and add mixture to empty squash halves. Sprinkle with mozzarella, Edam, and Parmesan cheeses. Bake until top is bubbling and browned, about 30 minutes.

Osso Buco

Osso buco is the most soul-satisfying dish I know; every ingredient is transformed through long, slow cooking. Use a heavy-bottomed brazier or Dutch oven with a tight-fitting lid. Serve with Sweet Corn Polenta (p. 100).

MAKES 4 SERVINGS

4 veal shanks

1 tsp kosher salt

½ tsp ground black pepper

3 tbsp extra virgin olive oil

1 cup (250 mL) diced onions

2 carrots, sliced in thick rounds

1 cup (250 mL) diced celery

2 tbsp all-purpose flour

3 cups (750 mL) low-sodium chicken or vegetable stock

½ cup (125 mL) white wine

3 tbsp tomato paste

4 fresh bay leaves

2 tbsp fresh thyme leaves

3 tbsp chopped fresh parsley

If you aren't crazy about the idea of eating veal, ease your mind by making this dish with beef, bison, lamb, or venison shanks.

Preheat oven to 250°F (120°C).

Rub shanks with salt and pepper. In a large oven-proof pot on medium, heat olive oil until just smoking. Add shanks and brown on all sides. Remove shanks from pot and set aside. To pot, add onions, carrots, and celery, and sauté until softened, about 5 minutes. Add flour and stir to coat vegetables. Add stock, wine, and tomato paste and stir until thick sauce forms. Add bay leaves and thyme. Return shanks to bottom of pan.

Cover pot with lid and bake for 3 hours. Remove and discard bay leaves. Sprinkle parsley over shanks before serving.

Moroccan Lamb with Squash

This hearty stew is traditionally made in a clay vessel called a tagine. Tagine dishes are often meat and vegetable concoctions with a spicy or pungent twist such as Moroccan olives, harissa paste, or preserved lemons. Serve with couscous or Rice Pilaf (p. 55).

MAKES 4 SERVINGS

1 lb (500 g) lamb stew meat

1 tsp kosher salt

1 tbsp Ras-el-hanout or garam masala

2 tsp harissa paste

2 tbsp extra virgin olive oil

4 garlic cloves, minced

1 cup (250 mL) diced onions

20 strands saffron or about ½ tsp ground

3 cups (750 mL) butternut squash, chopped

¼ cup (60 mL) pitted Moroccan olives

1 tbsp minced preserved lemon

Ras-el-hanout is a spice mixture found in Tunisian, Algerian, and Moroccan cuisine. It contains ground cumin and coriander seeds, turmeric, ginger, cardamom, and nutmeg, among other spices.

Preheat oven to 325°F (160°C).

In a bowl, mix lamb, salt, Ras-el-hanout, and harissa. In a large pot or Dutch oven on medium, heat olive oil. Sauté garlic and onions until lightly browned, about 5 minutes. Add lamb mixture and cook until browned, about 5 minutes.

Add saffron and enough water to almost cover lamb. Bring to a boil, cover with a lid, and bake for 45 minutes. Add squash and bake for another 30 minutes. Stir in olives and preserved lemon and bake for 10 minutes.

Homemade Canadian Bacon

Of all the uses for garden-grown sage, bacon is my favorite. It is remarkably easy to make and people go nuts for fresh Canadian bacon. Brining bacon requires that you be able to store at least two entire pork loins in 1 gal (4 L) of liquid for two days. I use a food-grade cooler and make up half the volume of the brine with ice to keep things nice and cool. A turkey brining bag will do the trick, too.

Bacon requires one ingredient that can be challenging to acquire—it's not sold in grocery stores. Curing salt is known by a variety of names including pink salt, Prague Powder #1, and nitrite salt. You will need to go to a real butcher shop—the kind where they make sausage and bacon—and convince them you know how to use it. They will be reticent, but tell them you have a reputable recipe and instructions. Do not use curing salt for anything but charcuterie.

MAKES 8 POUNDS (3.5 KG)

1½ cups (375 mL) kosher salt

1 cup (250 mL) white sugar

2½ tbsp curing salt

12 fresh sage leaves

3 tbsp fresh thyme leaves

12 black peppercorns

4 garlic cloves

2 whole pork loins

In a large pot on high heat, bring 2 qt/L water to a boil. Add salt, sugar, and curing salt. Reduce heat to medium and stir until salt and sugar have dissolved. Add sage, thyme, and peppercorns. Lightly crush garlic with side of a knife. Don't worry about stalks and garlic skins; throw it all in. Turn off heat, cover pot with lid, and allow to cool for 2 hours. Place pot in refrigerator and thoroughly chill.

Trim fat and silver skin (see p. 148) from pork loin and cut meat into 6-in (15-cm) chunks. Place pork and brine in a food-grade container lined with a large brining bag. Top up with 1 qt/L water and ice cubes (for a total of 4 qt/L brining liquid). Keep cool for 48 hours. Rotate pork chunks every 12 hours to ensure even brine absorption.

After 2 days, remove pork and discard brine. Rinse pork under cold water and set on a wire rack over a cookie sheet. Place rack and pork in refrigerator for 18 hours.

Preheat oven or smoker to 225°F (105°C). If using a smoker, apply 40 minutes of hickory or applewood smoke. Heat pork to internal temperature of 150°F (65°C), about 2½ hours. Remove from oven/smoker and allow to cool for 2 hours. Place bacon in freezer bags or vacuum seal and store in freezer for up to 6 months.

Homemade Party Pizzas

Pizza is one of those magic foods. It's as comfortable in a greasy slice shop as it is in posh eateries. (Thank you, Wolfgang Puck.) It's the quintessential party food, pleasing both to five-year-olds and to grandmothers. You can get a pizza stone for as little as $15—go buy one immediately.

MAKES 4 12-IN (30.5-CM) PIZZAS

DOUGH:

2 cups (500 mL) warm water

2 tbsp sugar

2 tbsp dry yeast

5 cups (1.25 L) all-purpose flour

1 tbsp kosher salt

1 tbsp dried oregano

1 tbsp dried basil

1 tsp dried thyme

3 tbsp (45 mL) extra virgin olive oil

flour, for kneading

olive oil, to coat bowl

General rules for pizza assembly: Dry meats (such as salami or pepperoni) and mushrooms go under the cheese, and wet vegetables and ham go on top, so moisture can escape. Nobody likes soggy pizza.

In a bowl, combine water and sugar, and stir until dissolved. Stir in yeast and set aside until it foams.

In a large mixing bowl, whisk together flour, salt, oregano, basil, and thyme. Add yeast mixture and olive oil to flour mixture. Mix until a dough forms. Flour a large working surface and turn dough out. Knead, adding flour as required, until dough is smooth and elastic, about 5 minutes. (A KitchenAid stand mixer

with a dough hook on medium speed does the job in about 2 minutes.) Coat inside of large bowl with 1 tsp olive oil and place dough inside. Cover bowl with wax paper or beeswax wrap and set in a warm location to rise for 1 hour.

Place a pizza stone on middle rack of oven. Preheat oven to 500°F (260°C). Place a sheet of parchment paper on a rimless baking sheet. (An upside-down cookie sheet will do.) Cut dough into 4 pieces. Dust working surface with flour. Roll 1 piece dough into a 12-in (30.5-cm) round. Lay it flat on parchment paper.

Apply toppings as instructed below. Slide dough and parchment paper carefully from baking sheet onto pizza stone. Bake pizza with toppings for 8–10 minutes, until cheese is lightly browned and bubbling. Carefully slide pizza from the pizza stone back onto baking sheet, then transfer it onto a cutting board. Hold edge of pizza and gently tug parchment paper from under crust. Slice into wedges.

Here are 2 of my favorite combinations. Each makes enough for a 12-in (30.5-cm) pizza.

PESTO PIZZA:

½ cup (125 mL) Basil Pesto (p. 76)

1 cup (250 mL) grated mozzarella cheese

½ cup (125 mL) grated Edam cheese

Spread pesto evenly over pizza dough, leaving ½ in (1 cm) bare around edges. Cover evenly with mozzarella, then Edam. Bake as directed above.

DELUXE PIZZA:

½ cup (125 mL) Arrabiata Sauce (p. 156)

10 slices pizza pepperoni

½ cup (125 mL) sliced fresh mushrooms

1 cup (250 mL) grated mozzarella cheese

½ cup (125 m) grated Edam cheese

¼ cup (60 mL) diced onions

¼ cup (60 mL) diced green bell peppers

3 tbsp sliced olives

Spread Arrabiata sauce evenly over dough, leaving ½ in (1 cm) bare around edges. Lay pepperoni and mushrooms evenly over sauce. Cover evenly with mozzarella, then Edam. Sprinkle onions, peppers, and olives over cheese. Bake as directed above.

Homemade Ricotta (p. 199)

Vegetarian Zucchini Lasagna

I started experimenting with vegetarian lasagna while working as a staff cook for a ski hill. My crew was a collection of surprisingly athletic Albertan head bangers, BC ski bums, and Australian drifters who lived in the staff residence. They devoured this with animal intensity. This version is both meat-free and low-carb. Use young tender zucchini, so you can leave the skin on.

MAKES 6 SERVINGS

SAUCE:

2 tbsp extra virgin olive oil

1½ cups (375 mL) diced onions

4 garlic cloves, minced

1 green bell pepper, diced

1 carrot, peeled and finely grated

1 medium zucchini, coarsely grated

6 fresh basil leaves

2 tbsp fresh oregano

1 tsp fresh thyme leaves

1 tbsp chopped fresh rosemary

3 cups (750 mL) crushed tomatoes

¼ cup (60 mL) chopped flat-leaf parsley

2 tsp kosher salt

½ tsp black pepper

LASAGNA:

2 cups (500 mL) Homemade Ricotta (p. 199)
   or cottage cheese

2 large eggs

½ cup (125 mL) chopped fresh herbs (mix of
   basil, parsley, marjoram, oregano)

½ cup (125 mL) grated Parmesan cheese

2 medium zucchinis, sliced lengthwise to
   ¼-in (6-mm) strips

8 dried oven-ready lasagna noodles

3 cups (750 mL) fresh baby spinach leaves

2 cups (500 mL) grated mozzarella cheese

½ cup (125 mL) grated provolone cheese

½ cup (125 mL) grated Edam cheese

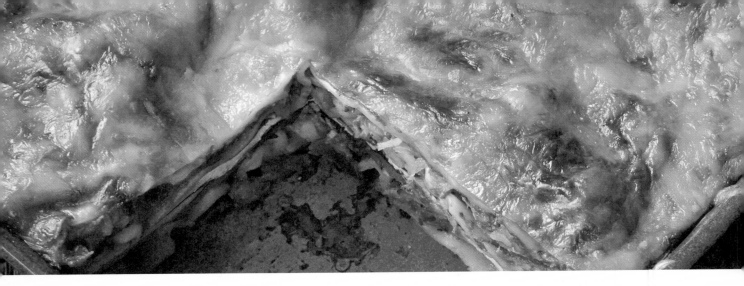

Wait until you are ready to bake the lasagna before you assemble it. If you put it together in advance, the noodles will turn to a floury mush.

Preheat oven to 350°F (180°C).

In a large saucepan on medium, heat olive oil. Sauté onions until translucent, about 3 minutes. Add garlic, bell peppers, carrots, and zucchini and cook until soft, about 5 minutes. Stir in basil, oregano, thyme, rosemary, tomatoes, and parsley. Increase heat to medium-high and bring to a low boil. Add salt and pepper, reduce heat to low, and simmer uncovered until thickened, about 60 minutes. Taste and season with salt and pepper, if desired. (You can be a little heavy on the salt, as this sauce will also season noodles and zucchini slices.)

In a bowl, combine ricotta, eggs, chopped herb mixture, and Parmesan. Set ricotta mixture aside. Spread 1 ladle sauce in bottom of a deep 9 x 12-in (23 x 30.5-cm) baking dish or foil lasagna pan. Place zucchini slices over sauce. Add 2 more ladles of sauce. Cover with 4 dried oven-ready lasagna noodles. Spoon ricotta mixture over noodles and spread evenly. Lay spinach leaves over ricotta layer and cover with another layer of zucchini. Gently compress layers, to make space. Add 2 more ladles sauce and another layer of pasta. Ladle on remainder of the sauce and cover with mozzarella, then sprinkle provolone and Edam evenly over top.

Bake for 60 minutes or until browned and bubbling. Rest for 30 minutes before slicing.

Homemade Ricotta Cheese

Try this once, and you will never look at commercially made cottage cheese the same way again. Watch your friends' faces when you casually mention, "The cheese? Oh, I made it this morning."

MAKES 2 CUPS (500 ML) CURDS

8 cups (2 L) whole milk

1 cup (250 mL) cream

1 tsp kosher salt

3 tbsp lemon juice

The temperature of the milk mixture is tremendously important. If it isn't at a rolling simmer, the chemistry won't work. Also, once it reaches temperature, the mixture may boil over quickly, so be on your toes.

Line a colander set in the sink or over a pot with two layers of cheesecloth.

In a large saucepan on medium-low heat, slowly bring milk and cream to a simmer, then add salt. Increase heat to medium-high and bring mixture to a low rolling boil. Add lemon juice and turn off heat, but leave on burner. Stir for 1 minute as curds form, then pour mixture into cheesecloth-lined colander. Let curds drain for 30 minutes.

Darcy's Donkey-Kickin' Macaroni & Cheese

Mac and cheese may not be the most heart-healthy meal you can eat, but life requires balance. Sometimes that means eating something for pure pleasure, though this one has the redeeming addition of fresh vegetables. Over the years, we have embellished the recipe to achieve the most intense cheese flavor imaginable. Enjoy.

MAKES 4–6 SERVINGS

3 cups (750 mL) broccoli florets

1 tbsp olive oil

¼ cup (60 mL) chopped prosciutto

6 tbsp butter

6 tbsp all-purpose flour

3 cups (750 mL) milk

½ tsp white pepper

2 cups (500 mL) grated cheddar cheese, divided

1 cup (250 mL) grated provolone cheese

1 cup (250 mL) grated Gruyère cheese

½ cup (125 mL) MacLaren's Imperial sharp cheddar or extra-sharp cheese spread

2 tsp Dijon mustard

2 tsp Louisiana-style hot sauce

1 lb (500 g) dried macaroni

½ cup (125 mL) fresh peas

Preheat oven to 375°F (190°C).

In a large pot on high heat, boil 4 qt/L of water. Add broccoli and blanch for 1 minute. Remove broccoli and immerse in cold water. Set aside.

In a frying pan on medium-high, heat oil. Fry prosciutto until crisp, about 3 minutes. Set prosciutto aside.

In a large saucepan on medium-low heat, melt butter and stir in flour. Cook until fragrant, about 2 minutes. Remove saucepan from heat for 2 minutes.

In a microwave oven, warm milk gently until tepid, then add to flour mixture and whisk until smooth. Place saucepan back on medium-high heat, add pepper, and stir until it thickens. Reduce heat to medium-low. Add 1 cup (250 mL) each cheddar, provolone, and Gruyère, a handful at a time, stirring until melted. Crumble in Imperial cheddar, stirring gently until melted. Stir in mustard and hot sauce.

In a large pot on high heat, bring 6 qt/L water and 2 tbsp salt to a boil. Add macaroni and cook until tender but firm. Drain macaroni and transfer to a large baking dish. Add cheese sauce, prosciutto, broccoli, and peas and stir to combine. Top with 1 cup (250 mL) cheddar and bake for 25 minutes, until top is browned and bubbling.

Hoppin' John

Here's my take on Hoppin' John, a traditional southern side dish and a great source of fiber and vitamins. It's also the most intensely comforting thing you can eat on a rainy day. If you don't have collards, make this dish with kale, turnip greens, or mustard tops.

Note: Soak black-eyed peas the night before you make this dish.

MAKES 6–8 SERVINGS

2 tbsp extra virgin olive oil

1 cup (250 mL) diced onions

½ (125 mL) cup diced celery

¾ cup (185 mL) diced tomatoes

2 garlic cloves, minced

2 fresh bay leaves

1 tbsp Randy's All-Purpose Seasoning (p.119)

3 cups (750 mL) chopped collard greens

1 small ham hock

1 cup (250 mL) dried black-eyed peas, soaked overnight

1 cup (250 mL) basmati rice

1 roasted red bell pepper (p. 45), diced

1 cup (250 mL) chopped green onions

In a large heavy-bottomed saucepan such as a Dutch oven on medium, heat olive oil. Add onions, celery, tomatoes, garlic, bay leaves, and All-Purpose Seasoning. Sauté until vegetables soften, about 5 minutes. Add collards and turn until wilted. Add ham hock, soaked black-eyed peas, and enough water to barely cover other ingredients, but not less than 4 cups (1 L). Increase heat to high and bring to a boil. Cover with a lid, reduce heat to low, and simmer for 1 hour. Remove lid and simmer for 1 more hour. Ensure that at least 2 cups (500 mL) liquid remain and add more water if needed.

Remove ham hock and shred meat, discarding bone and skin. Remove bay leaves and discard. Add rice to pot and bring to a boil, cover with a lid, and reduce heat to low for 10 minutes. Turn off heat and let pot sit covered on burner for another 20 minutes. Return meat to pot. Stir in roasted red peppers and green onions.

Smothered Green Beans

If you know a local full-service hog farmer or butcher, chances are she will have smoked ham hocks. This is slow-food nirvana: tender green beans with flaked ham and pot liquor so good you'll sneak a shooter.

MAKES 8 SERVINGS

2 tbsp extra virgin olive oil

1 medium ham hock

1 medium onion

½ tsp ground black pepper

2 lb (1 kg) green beans, trimmed

salt, to taste

ground black pepper, to taste

In a large pot over medium, heat olive oil. Sear ham hock on one side for about 3 minutes. Turn ham hock and add onions and pepper. Sauté onions until softened, about 5 minutes. Add green beans and push them down with a spoon. Add just enough water to almost cover green beans.

Increase heat to high and bring to a boil. Cover with a lid, reduce heat to low, and simmer for 1 hour. Remove lid and simmer for 1 more hour.

Remove ham hock and set aside to cool. Remove meat from ham hock and discard skin and bone. Add meat to pot and adjust seasoning with salt and pepper, if desired.

Green Bean Mushroom Bake

This is a delicious home-made version of a green bean casserole that always has a place in our Christmas dinner. Water chestnuts and almonds give it a nice light crunch. Most recipes call for cans of soup, tins of crispy fried onions, and other processed foods. This version is tastier, lower in sodium, and more wholesome.

MAKES 6–8 SERVINGS

¼ cup (60 mL) unsalted butter

1 cup (250 mL) diced onions

2 cups (500 mL) sliced white mushrooms

1½ tsp kosher salt

½ tsp ground black pepper

2 tbsp sherry

¼ cup (60 mL) all-purpose flour

1 cup (250 mL) low-sodium or Homemade chicken (p. 176) or turkey (p. 212) stock

1 cup (250 mL) whipping cream

1¼ cups (310 mL) grated cheddar cheese, divided

2 pounds (1 kg) green beans, trimmed and chopped

1 8-oz (227-mL) tin sliced water chestnuts, drained

¼ cup (60 mL) blanched slivered almonds

Preheat oven to 325°F (160°C).

In a large saucepan on medium heat, melt butter. Sauté onions for 5 minutes, until soft. Add mushrooms, salt, and pepper, and sauté until mushrooms are cooked, about 3 minutes. Add sherry and reduce for 2 minutes. Stir in flour to make a paste.

In the microwave or a small saucepan on medium-low, warm stock and cream until tepid and add to saucepan, stirring until very thick, about 3–5 minutes. Remove from heat and stir in ¼ cup (60 mL) cheese, green beans, water chestnuts, and almonds. Place mixture in a ceramic baking dish and sprinkle with 1 cup (250 mL) cheddar cheese.

Cover dish with a lid or foil and bake for 30 minutes. Bake uncovered for another 15 minutes.

Parmesan Turnip Croquettes

Turnips can be a tough sell, especially with kids. You can put them in stews where they are just one voice in the chorus, but on their own, turnips need a bit of help. Enter the croquette. Serve with Basil Garlic Dip (p. 79).

MAKES 10 CROQUETTES

1 large turnip

1 cup (250 mL) bread crumbs

6 tbsp grated Parmesan cheese, divided

1 tsp kosher salt

¼ tsp ground black pepper

2 egg yolks

1 egg white

1 large egg

2–3 cups (500–750 mL) canola oil, for frying

Peel turnip and cut into chunks. In a separate saucepan fitted with a steamer rack on high heat, steam turnip for 15 minutes, until completely tender. Drain, then mash. Place mashed turnip on two layers of cheesecloth, wrap, and wring out liquid.

In a mixing bowl, thoroughly combine 1 cup (250 mL) turnip pulp, 2 tbsp bread crumbs, 3 tbsp Parmesan cheese, salt, pepper, and egg yolks.

In a separate bowl, whisk 1 egg white with whole egg. On a plate, combine remainder of cheese and bread crumbs. Roll 1½ tbsp turnip mixture into a ball, dredge in bread crumb mixture, and let stand for 10 minutes. Dip each ball in egg mixture, then dredge again in bread crumb mixture. Refrigerate 1 hour.

In a medium saucepan, preheat canola oil to 350°F (180°C). Fill pot no more than halfway with oil. Fry croquettes in batches of 5 until browned, about 2–3 minutes. Be careful when working with hot oil! Remove croquettes and drain on a paper towel. Serve hot.

Collard Greens with Roasted Red Pepper

My vegetarian version of this usually meaty southern classic requires only the bounty of your garden and takes half the standard cooking time. Feel free to substitute beet greens or turnip tops for some or all of the collard greens. Serve beside grilled meat or Darcy's Donkey-Kickin' Macaroni and Cheese (p. 200).

MAKES 6–8 SERVINGS

12 large collard green leaves

2 tbsp canola oil

1 medium onion, thinly sliced

2 garlic cloves, peeled and mashed flat

2 tbsp Randy's All-Purpose Seasoning (p. 119)

1 roasted red bell pepper (p. 45), diced

Remove stems from collards and discard. Slice leaves into 1-in (2.5-cm) strips. In a large pot on medium, heat oil. Sauté onions and garlic for 5 minutes.

Add All-Purpose Seasoning and stir for 1 minute. Increase heat to high and add 3 cups (750 mL) water and collard greens. Bring to a boil and turn greens until wilted. Push collards down with a spoon to immerse in cooking liquid and reduce heat to low.

Cover pot and simmer for 1 hour. Add roasted red pepper and simmer for another 5 minutes.

Singapore Curry Sauce with Kale

I like to serve this creamy, rich sauce with Beer-Battered Fish (p. 183), but don't stop there. You can also poach chicken breasts or Turkey Meatballs (p. 187) in this coconut-based sauce, or go meatless and use squares of firm tofu. Serve with rice.

MAKES 4 SERVINGS

1 tbsp canola oil

2 tbsp grated fresh ginger

2 garlic cloves, minced

1 jalapeño pepper, seeded and minced

½ cup (125 mL) minced shallots

3 tbsp curry powder

½ tbsp ground cumin

½ tbsp ground coriander

½ tsp ground turmeric

3 tbsp tomato paste

2 14-oz (398-mL) cans coconut milk

1–2 tsp kosher salt, to taste

3 cups (750 mL) chopped lacinato kale

Beer-Battered Fish, Turkey Meatballs, or tofu

¼ cup (60 mL) cilantro leaves

In a large sauté pan on medium, heat canola oil. Sauté ginger, garlic, jalapeño, and shallots until softened, about 5 minutes. Add curry powder, cumin, coriander, turmeric, and tomato paste and stir to combine. Stir in coconut milk and salt, and bring to a low simmer. Stir in kale and simmer for 15 minutes.

Add turkey meatballs (or fish, chicken breasts, tofu squares) and simmer until heated through. Alternately, serve topped with Beer-Battered Fish. Garnish with cilantro leaves.

Nut Flour Waffles

If you have a food processor, you can make all kinds of flour mixes, adding whichever grains, cereals, or nuts you like. This batter works for both waffles and pancakes. Top with any combination of butter, syrup, nuts, and sliced bananas.

MAKES 5–6 BELGIAN WAFFLES

⅓ cup (80 mL) walnut halves

⅓ cup (80 mL) pecan halves

½ cup (125 mL) whole wheat flour

1 cup (250 mL) all-purpose flour

1 tsp kosher salt

4 tsp baking powder

1 tsp ground cinnamon

⅛ tsp ground nutmeg

2 large eggs

1½ (375 mL) cups milk

3 tbsp brown sugar

3 tbsp canola oil

Pecans are rich in antioxidants and may therefore play a role in improving heart and brain function. Walnuts are rich in healthy oils, fiber, vitamins, and minerals.

You can use nut flour in other types of baking; simply substitute it for up to half of the regular flour in almost any recipe.

Preheat waffle iron.

In a food processor, pulse walnuts, pecans, and whole wheat flour until mixture is smooth and fine. In a large bowl, whisk nut flour with all-purpose flour, salt, baking powder, cinnamon, and nutmeg to combine.

In a separate bowl, whisk eggs, milk, sugar, and canola oil. Add wet ingredients to dry and whisk until just combined. Let stand for 5 minutes. Ladle ⅔ cup (160 mL) batter onto waffle iron and cook according to manufacturer's instructions.

Christmas Dinner

After twenty years of preparing Christmas dinner, my spread has coalesced into a few traditional core recipes that are integrated for efficiency. The recipes for the brine, quick turkey stock, gravy, and even the compound butter are designed to be used together to create comforting flavors that run through the entire meal. Round out your holiday meal with Roasted Garlic Mashed Potatoes (p. 162) and Green Bean Mushroom Bake (p. 204).

The next day, turkey leftovers get a makeover into Boxing Day Soup (p. 218). Note: In Great Britain and Canada—and much of the former British Empire—the day after Christmas is celebrated with cleverly reimagined turkey leftovers and discount shopping.

Fragrant Turkey Brine

I remain skeptical of basting as a way to attain juicy breast meat. It seems to me that little if any moisture could penetrate the skin and subcutaneous fat that covers the white meat simply by pouring pan drippings over the bird. Certainly the juices contain enough fat to help the browning process, and that is a worthwhile exercise. But as a way to add moisture? No. Brining ensures a moist, flavorful turkey, and I swear it speeds up the cooking time as well.

MAKES 2 GALLONS (8 L)

1 gal (4 L) water

1 cup (250 mL) kosher salt

2 tsp black peppercorns

3 garlic cloves, lightly smashed

1 cup (250 mL) honey

1 bunch fresh flat-leaf parsley

1 bunch fresh thyme

2 6-in (15-cm) sprigs fresh rosemary

12 fresh sage leaves

5 fresh bay leaves

1 lemon or orange, halved

48 ice cubes

In a large saucepan on high heat, bring water to a boil. Add salt, peppercorns, garlic, honey, parsley, thyme, rosemary, sage, and bay leaves. Squeeze in lemon or orange and add both halves. Cover pan and turn off heat, allowing brine to steep and cool for several hours. Place in refrigerator to finish cooling.

In a 4 qt/L container, place ice cubes, and top up with cold water. In a large food-safe container or brining bag, combine ice water with brine. Submerge turkey in liquid for 4–24 hours.

Quick Turkey Neck Stock

Before roasting, the turkey donates its wings, neck, and gizzard to a stock that will ensure intense turkey flavor in the gravy and the stuffing.

MAKES ABOUT 6 CUPS (1.5 L)

1 turkey neck

1 turkey heart

1 turkey gizzard

2 turkey wing tips

1 onion, quartered, skin on

1 carrot, cut into chunks

1 tbsp extra virgin olive oil

½ tsp kosher salt

Preheat oven to 375°F (190°C).

Remove neck and organ meats from turkey cavity. Discard liver and bag. Using a very sharp knife, remove outer two joints from each turkey wing, leaving segment attached to turkey breast.

In a large metal roasting pan, place neck, heart, gizzard, and wing tips. Add onions and carrots. Drizzle with olive oil and sprinkle with salt. Bake for 30 minutes. Turn meats over for even browning. Roast for another 30 minutes, until meat has browned.

Fill a kettle with water and bring to a boil. In a large pot, place roasted meats and vegetables. Pour 2 cups (500 mL) boiling water into roaster. Using a wooden spoon, scrape up brown residue and pour mixture into soup pot. Add another 4 cups (1 L) water to pot. On medium-low heat, simmer stock for 1 hour. Strain and set stock aside for stuffing and gravy.

Thyme-Orange Compound Butter

Smear this flavorful butter over the skin of the turkey before roasting.
It's so good, you may also want to toss it with boiled carrots or
use it to top baked yams.

MAKES ABOUT ½ CUP (125 ML)

½ cup (125 mL) unsalted butter

2 tsp fresh thyme leaves

¼ tsp ground black pepper

zest of 1 orange

In a bowl, soften butter. Stir
in thyme, pepper, and zest and
mix to combine well. Mash
with a fork.

Farmhouse Stuffing

*This is the stuffing that folks have been making for generations.
It will infuse your turkey with all the aromas of the garden. The recipe is
very basic but open to all the imagination you can muster. Some years we add
crumbled sausage meat, other years, chopped fresh oysters. Slivered nuts or even
diced apples are also a welcome addition. (What about crumbled pork sausages
and diced apples? See how this works?) This version calls for the addition of
Quick Turkey Neck Stock (p. 212), but if you can't manage that, store-bought
low-sodium chicken stock will suffice. I don't judge.*

MAKES 12 SERVINGS

500 g white bread cubes

300 g multigrain bread cubes

¾ cup (185 mL) unsalted butter

4 cups (1 L) diced onions

3 cups (750 mL) diced celery

2 ½ cups (625 mL) sliced fresh white
  mushrooms

2 tsp kosher salt

1 tsp ground black pepper

1 cup (250 mL) chopped fresh parsley and
  stems

2 tbsp chopped fresh sage leaves

2 tbsp chopped fresh rosemary leaves

2 tbsp chopped fresh thyme

2 cups (500 mL) Quick Turkey Neck Stock
  (p. 212)

Break white and multigrain bread into chunks with your fingers and spread on a large baking sheet to dry, preferably a day or two before making stuffing.

Preheat oven to 325°F (160°C).

An hour before the turkey goes in the oven, place bread cubes into a large mixing bowl, leaving enough room to add vegetables and stock later. (You might need to split it between two bowls.)

In a large saucepan on medium heat, melt butter. Add onions, celery, mushrooms, salt, and pepper and sauté for 5 minutes, stirring occasionally. Add parsley, sage, rosemary, and thyme, stirring to mix evenly.

Pour vegetable mixture over bread cubes and toss to combine. Pour stock over mixture and toss again. When turkey is ready to go into oven, stuff as much mixture into cavity of turkey as you can.

Line a large baking dish with foil, enough to wrap foil over top. Place remainder of stuffing in baking dish, wrap foil over top, and place in refrigerator. One hour before dinner, place dish in oven and bake until internal temperature reaches 165°F (75°C).

Roast Turkey

*The centerpiece of a great holiday meal should look and smell amazing.
This bird delivers. Brining ensures that every bite is moist and delicious,
while the compound butter helps the skin brown and fills the
house with an undeniable Christmas aroma.*

MAKES 12 SERVINGS, WITH ENOUGH LEFTOVERS TO MAKE BOXING DAY SOUP (P. 218)

1 16-lb (7-kg) turkey

Fragrant Turkey Brine (p. 211)

Farmhouse Stuffing (p. 214)

Thyme-Orange Compound Butter (p. 213)

Helpful hints:

*Do not use a kosher
or Butterball turkey,
which are already
seasoned.*

*Do ensure that brine is
cold before the turkey
goes in.*

*Do not rinse the brine
off. The salt and sugar
will help the skin
brown.*

*Do let your turkey
warm to room tempera-
ture for 1 hour before
roasting.*

Brine turkey overnight in
Fragrant Turkey Brine.

Preheat oven to 325°F (160°C).

Remove turkey from brine,
towel dry, and move to a
large roasting pan. Fill cavity
of turkey with Farmhouse
Stuffing. Make a baseball-sized
ball of stuffing and place it
under neck flap skin, tucking
the skin under to hold it in
place. Use your hands to smear
skin with Thyme-Orange
Compound Butter.

Roast turkey until juices in leg
run clear when tested with a
fork or preferably to an internal temperature of 165°F
(75°C). *Note*: Stuffing inside
turkey must also reach 165°F
(75°C) to ensure that any
pathogens are rendered harm-
less. A brined turkey requires
12–15 minutes per pound. To
ensure even browning, turn
roaster every 45 minutes or so.
Remove turkey from roaster.
Cover with foil and a couple of
tea towels for 15–30 minutes
before carving.

Turkey Gravy

The combination of turkey stock and drippings make this gravy a virtual explosion of amazing turkey flavor. Making gravy is not rocket science but, in a way, it is chemistry. Gravy can and does go wrong, and for that reason cooks feel immense pressure to get it right. Relax. Math is hard, gravy is not. Only a tiny bit of effort is required to guarantee memorable gravy.

MAKES 12 SERVINGS

½ cup (125 mL) turkey fat from roasted turkey

½ cup (125 mL) all-purpose flour

4 cups (1 L) Quick Turkey Neck Stock, (p. 212)

¼ tsp white pepper

kosher salt

Remove turkey from roaster and set aside to rest. Pour liquid and fat from roaster into a bowl or gravy separator. It should soon separate into a water-based brown liquid on the bottom and lighter-colored oil on top. Use a ladle to remove fat to a separate bowl. Reserve pan juices.

There should be lots of "fond," rich brown bits stuck to the bottom of the roaster. Place roaster on burner on medium-low heat and add in ½ cup (125 mL) turkey fat. Add ½ cup (125 mL) flour and whisk until combined. Cook flour until aromatic and light brown in color.

Remove roaster from heat and let it cool for 2–3 minutes. Add 2 cups (500 mL) stock, gently scraping with a wooden spoon to remove fond. Add in pan juices from roaster. Return roaster to heat on low and add stock in ½-cup (125-mL) portions, whisking until it achieves a smooth consistency. Season to taste with white pepper and salt, if desired.

Simmer for 5 minutes.

When you are ready to serve, thin mixture with more stock, if necessary. If you want a really perfect looking sauce, pour it through a wire mesh sieve.

Boxing Day Soup

Boxing Day Soup is how Darcy and I turn Christmas Day's frenzy of feasting into a next-day cleanse. It also puts to immediate use the large pot of turkey stock we cooked after dinner the night before. We make this soup with star-shaped semolina noodles called stelline, but any small semolina pasta will work. However, our kids beg for Turkey and Stars, and yours will too.

MAKES 8 SERVINGS

2 tbsp extra virgin olive oil

2 cups (500 mL) diced onions

2 cups (500 mL) diced carrots

2 cups (500 mL) diced celery

2 tsp kosher salt

1 tsp fresh ground black pepper

1 tsp fresh thyme leaves

½ cup (125 mL) pinot grigio (or other dry white wine)

12 cups (3 L) turkey stock

½ lb (250 g) dried stelline pasta

1 cup (250 mL) diced green beans

3 cups (750 mL) cubed leftover turkey

parsley, for garnish

In a large pot on medium-low, heat olive oil. Add onions, carrots, celery, salt, pepper, and thyme and sauté, stirring occasionally until softened, about 5 minutes. Add wine and reduce for 3 minutes. Add stock, bring to a boil, and add pasta, stirring continuously for about 1 minute to prevent sticking.

Simmer for 10 minutes. Taste stock and adjust seasoning, if desired. Add green beans and turkey and simmer another 10 minutes. Garnish with parsley and serve with a turkey sandwich.

Index

Randy
Shore

PHOTO: Arlen Redekop

Randy Shore is a food and sustainability writer for the Vancouver Sun *and author of* The Green Man *blog; he is also a former restaurant cook and an avid gardener. He is a recipient of the BC and Yukon Community Newspaper Association Best Columnist Award and the BC Wildlife Federation Art Downs Award for conservation journalism. Randy and his wife Darcy grow as much of their own food as possible on an acre in Roberts Creek on BC's Sunshine Coast, creating new recipes and customizing familiar ones based on what the seasons bring.*

vancouversun.com/greenman